ACCEPTING THE UNIVERSE

BY

JOHN BURROUGHS

BOSTON AND NEW YORK

HOUGHTON MIFFLIN COMPANY

The Riverside Press Cambridge

1920

160

.... *And heard great argument*
About it and about : but evermore
Came out by the same door wherein I went.

THE RUBÁIYÁT

PREFACE

A WHEEL may have many spokes, but can have but one hub. So I may say of this volume of mine that there are many themes and chapter-headings, but there is but one central thought into which they all converge, and that is that the universe is good, and that it is our rare good fortune to form a part of it. As this collection of essays does not aim to be a systematic treatise on any one theme, but rather a series of sallies, excursions, into the world of semi-philosophical speculation, there is inevitably much repetition; there may even be some contradiction. But I have concluded to let them stand, as I find myself an interested spectator of the workings of my own mind when, in following different roads, it arrives at the same truth. As all roads lead to Rome, so in the realm in which my mind works in this volume, all roads lead to the conclusion that this is the best possible world, and these people in it are the best possible people.

The heart of Nature is sound. I feel toward the great Mother somewhat as a man does who takes out a policy in an insurance company: he believes the company is solvent and will meet its obligations. I look upon the universe as solvent and worthy of

vii

PREFACE

trust. In other words this is a book of radical optimism. It might be described as an attempt to justify the ways of God to man on natural grounds.

My reader need hardly be told that theological grounds do not count with me. I want nothing less than a faith founded upon a rock, faith in the constitution of things. The various man-made creeds are fictitious, like the constellations — Orion, Cassiopeia's Chair, the Big Dipper; the only thing real in them is the stars, and the only thing real in the creeds is the soul's aspiration toward the Infinite. This abides, though creeds and dogmas change or vanish.

Empedocles says:

> "O, wretched he whose care
> Is shadowy speculation on the gods."

But is not speculation better than indifference? Curiosity about the gods may lead to a better acquaintance with them. I feel that each of these chapters might be called an altar to the Unknown God.

JOHN BURROUGHS

CONTENTS

CONTENTS

The frontispiece, showing Mr. Burroughs at his woodpile at Riverby, is from a photograph taken in 1920 by Mr. HERBERT S. ARDELL

ACCEPTING THE UNIVERSE

I

SHALL WE ACCEPT THE UNIVERSE?

I

IT is reported of Margaret Fuller that she said
she accepted the universe. "Gad, she'd better!"
retorted Carlyle. Carlyle himself did not accept
the universe in a very whole-hearted manner. Looking up at the midnight stars, he exclaimed: "A sad
spectacle! If they be inhabited, what a scope for
misery and folly; if they be na inhabited, what a
waste of space!"

It ought not to be a hard thing to accept the
universe, since it appears to be a fixture, and we
have no choice in the matter; but I have found it
worth while to look the gift in the mouth, and convince myself that it is really worth accepting. It
were a pity to go through life with a suspicion in
one's mind that it might have been a better universe, and that some wrong has been done us because we have no freedom of choice in the matter.
The thought would add a tinge of bitterness to all
our days. And so, after living more than four score
years in the world, and pondering long and intently
upon the many problems which life and nature
present, I have come, like Margaret Fuller, to

accept the universe, have come frankly to accept that first verdict pronounced upon creation, namely, that it is very good — good in its sum total up to this astronomic date, whatever phases it may at times present that lead us to a contrary conclusion.

Not that cold and hunger, war and pestilence, tornadoes and earthquakes, are good in a positive sense, but that these and kindred things are vastly overbalanced by the forces and agencies that make for our well-being, — that "work together for good," — the sunshine, the cooling breezes, the fertile soil, the stability of land and sea, the gentle currents, the equipoise of the forces of the earth, air, and water, the order and security of our solar system, and, in the human realm, the good-will and fellowship that are finally bound to prevail among men and nations.

In remote geologic ages, before the advent of man, when the earth's crust was less stable, when the air was yet loaded with poisonous gases, when terrible and monstrous animal forms held high carnival in the sea and upon the land, it was not in the same sense good — good for beings constructed as we are now. In future astronomic time, when the earth's air and water and warmth shall have disappeared — a time which science predicts — and all life upon the globe fails, again it will not be good. But in our geologic, biologic, and astronomic age, notwithstanding the fact that cold and suffering, war and pestilence, cyclones and earthquakes, still occur upon the relatively tiny ball that carries us through the vast sidereal spaces, good is greatly in the ascendancy. The voyage is not all calm and sunshine, but it is safe, and the dangers from collision and shipwreck are very remote. It is a vast and lonely sea over which we are journeying, no other ships hail us and bid us Godspeed, no messages, wireless or other, may reach us from other shores, or other seas; forces and influences do play upon us from all parts of the empyrean, but, so far as we are aware, no living thing on other spheres takes note of our going or our coming.

In our practical lives we are compelled to separate good from evil — the one being that which favors our well-being, and the other that which antagonizes it; but, viewed as a whole, the universe is all good; it is an infinite complex of compensations out of which worlds and systems of worlds, and all which they hold, have emerged, and are emerging, and will emerge. This is not the language of the heart or of the emotions — our anthropomorphism cries out against it — but it is the language of serene, impartial reason. It is good for us occasionally to get outside the sphere of our personal life and view things as they are in and of themselves. A great demand is made upon our faith — faith in the absolute trustworthiness of human reason, and in the final beneficence of the forces that rule this universe. Not to solve the mysteries, but to see that they are insoluble, and to rest content in that conclusion, is the task we set ourselves here.

Evidently the tide of life is still at the flood on this planet; its checks and counter-currents arise inevitably in a universe whose forces are always, and always must be, in unstable equilibrium.

The love of the Eternal for mankind, and for all other forms of life, is not a parental love — not the love of the mother for her child, or of the father for his son; it is more like the love which a general has for his army; he is to lead that army through hardships, through struggles, through sufferings, and through death, but he is leading it to victory. Many will perish that others may live; the battle is being won daily. Evolution has triumphed. It has been a long and desperate battle, but here we are and we find life sweet. The antagonistic forces which have been overcome have become sources of power. The vast army of living forms moving down the geologic ages has been made strong through the trials and obstacles it has surmounted, till now we behold it in the fullness of its power with man at its head.

II

THERE is a paragraph in Emerson's Journal on Providence, written when he was twenty-one, which is as broad and as wise and as heterodox as anything he ever wrote. The Providence he depicts is the Providence I see in Nature:

"Providence supports, but does not spoil its children. We are called sons, not darlings, of the Deity. There is ever good in store for those who love it; knowledge for those who seek it; and if we do evil, we suffer the consequences of evil. Throughout the administration of the world there is the same aspect of stern kindness; of good against your will; good against your good; ten thousand channels of active beneficence, but all flowing with the same regard to general, not particular profit. . . . And to such an extent is this great statute policy of God carried, that many, nay, most, of the great blessings of humanity require cycles of a thousand years to bring them to their height."

A remarkable statement to be made in 1824, in New England, and by a fledgling preacher of the orthodox faith and the descendant of a long line of orthodox clergymen. It is as broad and as impartial as science, and yet makes a strong imaginative appeal. Good at the heart of Nature is the purport of it, not the patent-right good of the creeds, but good, free to all who love it, a "stern kindness," and no partial, personal, vacillating Providence whose ear is open only to the password of some sect or cult, or organization — "good against your good," your copyrighted good, your personal, selfish good (unless it is in line with equal good to others), the broad,

universal beneficence of Nature which brought us
here and keeps us here, and showers its good upon
us as long as we keep in right relations with it; but
which goes its appointed way regardless of the sore
needs of warring nations or the desperate straits of
struggling men. That is the Providence that lasts,
that does not change its mind, that is not indulgent,
that does not take sides, that is without variableness or shadow of turning. Suppose the law of
gravity were changeable, or the law of chemical reactions, or the nature of fire, or air, or water, or
cohesion? Gravity never sleeps nor varies, yet see
bodies rise, see others fall, see the strong master of
the weak, see the waters flow and the ground stay.
The laws of fluids are fixed, but see the variety of
their behavior, the forms in which they crystallize,
their solvent power, their stability or instability,
their capacity to absorb or conduct heat — flux
and change everywhere amid fixity and law. Nature
is infinitely variable, which opens the door to all
forms of life; her goings and comings are on such a
large scale, like the rains, the dews, the sunlight, that
all creatures get an equal benefit. She sows her seed
with such a generous hand that enough of them
are bound to fall upon fertile places. Such as are
very limited in range, like those of the swamp plants,
are yet cast forth upon the wind so liberally that
sooner or later some of them fall upon conditions
suitable to them. Nature will cover a whole town-

ship with her wind-sown seeds in order to be
sure that she hits the small swamp in one corner
of it.

A stream of energy, not described by the adjective "inexhaustible," bears the universe along,
and all forms of life, man with the rest, take their
chances amid its currents and its maelstroms. The
good Providence shows itself in the power of adaptation which all forms of life possess. Some forms of
sea-weed or sea-grass grow where the waves pound
the shore incessantly. How many frail marine creatures are wrecked upon the shore, but how many
more are not wrecked! How many ships go down
in the sea, but how many more are wafted safely
over it!

The Providence in Nature seems intent only on
playing the game, irrespective of the stakes, which to
us seem so important. Whatever the issue, Nature
is the winner. She cannot lose. Her beneficence is
wholesale. Her myriad forms of life are constantly
passing through "the curtain of fire" of her inorganic forces, and the casualties are great, but the
majority get through. The assault goes on and will
ever go on. It is like a stream of water that is whole
and individual at every point, but fixed and stable
at no point. To play the game, to keep the currents
going — from the depths of sidereal space to the
shallow pool by the roadside; from the rise and fall
of nations, to the brief hour of the minute summer

9

insects, the one overarching purpose seems to be to give free rein to life, to play one form against another, to build up and tear down, to gather together and to scatter — no rest, no end, nothing final — rocks decaying to build more rocks, worlds destroyed to build more worlds, nations disintegrating to build more nations, organisms perishing to feed more organisms, life playing into the hands of death everywhere, and death playing into the hands of life, sea and land interchanging, tropic and arctic meeting and mingling, day and night, winter and summer chasing each other over the earth — what a spectacle of change, what a drama never completed! Vast worlds and systems in fiery flux; one little corner of the cosmos teeming with life, vast areas of it, like Saturn and Jupiter, dead and barren through untold millions of years; collisions and disruptions in the heavens, tornadoes and earthquakes and wars and pestilence upon the earth — surely it all sounds worse than it is, for we are all here to see and contemplate the great spectacle; it sounds worse than it is to us because we are a part of the outcome of all these raging and conflicting forces. Whatever has failed, we have succeeded, and the beneficent forces are still coming our way. As I write these lines I see my neighbor and his boys gathering the hay from the meadows and building it into a great stack beside their glutted barns. I see a chipmunk carrying stores to his den, I see butterflies dancing by on painted wings, I see and hear the happy birds, and the August sun beams his best upon all the land.

The greatest of human achievements and the most precious is that of the great creative artist. In words, in color, in sounds, in forms, man comes nearest to emulating the Creative Energy itself. It seems as if the pleasure and the purpose of the Creative Energy were endless invention — to strike out new forms, to vary perpetually the pattern. She presents myriads of forms, myriads of types, inexhaustible variety in air, earth, water, ten thousand ways to achieve the same end, a prodigality of means that bewilders the mind; her aim to produce something new and different, an endless variety of forms that fly, that swim, that creep, in the sea, in the air, on the earth, in the fields, in the woods, on the shore. How many ways Nature has of scattering her seeds, how many types of wings, of hooks, of springs! In some she offers a wage to bird or quadruped in the shape of fruit, others she forcibly attaches to the passer-by. In all times and places there is a riot of invention.

III

ARE we not men enough to face things as they are? Must we be cosseted a little? Can we not be weaned from the old theological pap? Can we not rest content in the general beneficence of Nature's Provi-

dence? Must you and I have a special hold upon the
great Mother's apron strings?

I see the Nature Providence going its impartial
way. I see drought and flood, heat and cold, war
and pestilence, defeat and death, besetting man at
all times, in all lands. I see hostile germs in the air
he breathes, in the water he drinks, in the soil he
tills. I see the elemental forces as indifferent toward him as toward ants and fleas. I see pain and
disease and defeat and failure dogging his footsteps.
I see the righteous defeated and the ungodly triumphant — this and much more I see; and yet I
behold through the immense biological vista behind us the race of man slowly — oh, so slowly! —
emerging from its brute or semi-human ancestry
into the full estate of man, from blind instinct and
savage passion into the light of reason and moral
consciousness. I behold the great scheme of evolution unfolding despite all the delays and waste and
failures, and the higher forms appearing upon the
scene. I see on an immense scale, and as clearly as in
a demonstration in a laboratory, that good comes
out of evil; that the impartiality of the Nature Providence is best; that we are made strong by what we
overcome; that man is man because he is as free to
do evil as to do good; that life is as free to develop
hostile forms as to develop friendly; that power
waits upon him who earns it; that disease, wars,
the unloosened, devastating elemental forces, have

each and all played their part in developing and hardening man and giving him the heroic fiber. The good would have no tang, no edge, no cutting quality without evil to oppose it. Life would be tasteless or insipid, without pain and struggle and disappointment. Behold what the fiery furnace does for the metals — welding or blending or separating or purifying them, and behold the hell of contending and destructive forces out of which the earth came, and again behold the grinding and eroding forces, the storms and earthquakes and eruptions and disintegrations that have made it the green inhabitable world that now sustains us! No, the universal processes do not need disinfecting; the laws of the winds, the rains, the sunlight do not need rectifying. "I do not want the constellations any nearer," says Whitman. I do not want the natural Providence any more attentive. The celestial laws are here underfoot and our treading upon them does not obliterate or vulgarize them. Chemistry is incorruptible and immortal, it is the handmaid of God; the yeast works in the elements of our bread of life while we sleep; the stars send their influences, the earth renews itself, the brooding heaven gathers us under its wings, and all is well with us if we have the heroic hearts to see it.

In the curve of the moon's or of the planets' disks, all broken or irregular lines of the surface are lost to the eye — the wholeness of the sphere form subordinates and obliterates them all: so all the failures and cross-purposes and disharmonies in nature and life do not suffice to break or mar the ʽvast general beneficence; the flowing universal good is obvious above all.

So long as we think of the Eternal in terms of our experience — of the knowledge of concrete things and beings which life discloses to us — we are involved in contradictions. The ancients visualized their gods and goddesses — Jove, Apollo, Minerva, Juno, and all the others. Shall we do this for the Eternal and endow it with personality? Into what absurdities this leads us! The unspeakable, the unseeable, the unthinkable, the inscrutable, and yet the most obvious fact that life yields to us! Nearer and more vital than our own bodies, than our own parents, and yet eluding our grasp; vehemently denied, passionately accepted, scoffed, praised, feared, worshiped, giving rise to deism, atheism, pantheism, to idolatry, to persecution, to martyrdom, the great Reality in which we live and move and have our being, and yet for that very reason, because it is a part of us, or rather we are a part of it, are we unable to define it or seize it as a reality apart from ourselves. Our denial proves it; just as we use gravity to overcome gravity, so we use God to deny God. Just as pure light is of no color, but split up makes all the colors that we see, so God divided and reflected makes all the half-gods we worship in life. Green and blue and red and orange are not in the objects that reflect them, but are an experience of the eye. We might with our tongues deny the air, but our spoken words prove it. We cannot lift ourselves over the fence by our own waistbands; no more can we by searching find God, because He is not an object that has place and form and limitations. He is the fact of the fact, the life of the life, the soul of the soul, the incomprehensible, the sum of all contradictions, the unit of all diversity; he who knows Him, knows Him not; he who is without Him, is full of Him; turn your back upon Him, then turn your back upon gravity, upon air, upon light. He cannot be seen, but by Him all seeing comes. He cannot be heard, yet by Him all hearing comes. He is not a being, yet apart from Him there is no being — there is no apart from Him. We contradict ourselves when we deny Him; it is ourselves we deny, and equally do we contradict ourselves when we accept Him; it is something apart from ourselves which we accept.

When half-gods go, says Emerson, the gods arrive. But half-gods never go; we can house and entertain no other. What can we do with the Infinite, the Eternal? We can only deal with things in time and space — things that can be numbered and measured. What can we do with the infinitely little, the infinitely great? All our gods are half-gods made in our own image. No surer does the wax take the imprint of the seal than does the Infinite take the imprint of our finite minds. We create a Creator, we rule a Ruler, we invent a heaven and hell; they are laws of our own being, seen externally.

How, then, shall we adjust our lives to the conception of a universal, non-human, non-finite, algebraic God? They adjust themselves. Do your work, deal justly, love rightness, make the most of yourself, cherish the good, the beautiful, the true, practice the Christian and the heathen virtues of soberness, meekness, reverence, charity, unselfishness, justice, mercy, singleness of purpose; obey the commandments, the Golden Rule, imbue your spirit with the wisdom of all ages, for thus is the moral order of the world upheld.

The moral order and the intellectual order go hand in hand. Upon one rests our relation to our fellows, upon the other rests our relation to the cosmos.

We must know, and we must love; we must do, and we must enjoy; we must warm judgment with feeling, and illume conscience with reason.

Admit, if we must, that we are in the grip of a merciless power, that outside of our own kind there is nothing that shows us mercy or consideration, that the Nature of which we form a part goes her own way regardless of us; yet let us keep in mind that the very fact that we are here and find life good is proof that the mercilessness of Nature has not been inconsistent with our permanent well-being. The fact that flowers bloom and fruit and grains ripen, that the sun shines, that the rain falls, that food nourishes us, that love warms us, that evolution has brought us thus far on our way, that our line of descent has survived all the hazards of the geologic ages, all point to the fact that we are on the winning side, that our well-being is secured in the constitution of things. For all the cataclysms and disruptions, the globe has ripened on the great sidereal tree, and has become the fit abode of its myriad forms of life. Though we may be run down and crushed by the great terrestrial forces about us, just as we may be run down and crushed in the street, yet these forces play a part in the activities that sustain us; without them we should not be here to suffer at their hands.

Our life depends from moment to moment upon the air we breathe, yet its winds and tempests may destroy us; it depends from day to day upon the water we drink, yet its floods may sweep us away. We walk and climb and work and move mountains by gravity, and yet gravity may break every bone in our bodies. We spread our sails to the winds and they become our faithful servitors, yet the winds may drive us into the jaws of the breakers. How are our lives bound up and identified with the merciless forces that surround us! Out of the heart of fate comes our freedom; out of the reign of death

17

comes our life; out of the sea of impersonal energy come our personalities; out of the rocks comes the soil that sustains us; out of the fiery nebulæ came the earth with its apple-blossoms and its murmuring streams; out of the earth came man. If the cosmic forces were not merciless, if they did not go their own way, if they made exceptions for you and me, if in them there *were* variableness and even a shadow of turning, the vast inevitable beneficence of Nature would vanish, and the caprice and uncertainty of man take its place. If the sun were to stand still for Joshua to conquer his enemies, there would be no further need for it to resume its journey. What I am trying to get rid of is the pitying and meddling Providence which our feeble faith and half-knowledge have enthroned above us. We need stronger meat than the old theology affords us. We need to contemplate the ways of a Providence that has not been subsidized; we need encouragement in our attitude of heroic courage and faith toward an impersonal universe; we need to have our petty anthropomorphic views of things shaken up and hung out in the wind to air. The universe is not a school-room on the Montessori lines, nor a benevolent institution run on the most modern improved plan. It is a work-a-day field where we learn from hard knocks, and where the harvest, not too sure, waits upon our own right arm.

II

MANIFOLD NATURE

FEW persons, I fancy, ever spend much time in thinking seriously of this vast, ever-present reality which we call Nature; what our true relations to it are, what its relations are to what we call God, or what God's relations are to it; whether God and Nature are two or one — God and Nature, or only Nature, or only God.

When we identify Nature with God we are at once in sore straits because Nature has a terrible side to her, but the moment we separate God from Nature we are still more embarrassed. We create a hiatus which we must find something to fill. We must invent a Devil upon whom to saddle the evil that everywhere dogs the footsteps of the good. So we have both a God and a Devil, or two gods, on our hands contending with each other. Even our good friends in the churches talk glibly of the God of Nature, or Nature's God, little heeding the terrible black depths that lie under their words.

The Nature that the poets sing and that nature-writers exploit is far from being the whole story. When we think of Nature as meaning only birds and flowers and summer breezes and murmuring streams, we have only touched the hem of her garment — a garment that clothes the whole world with the terrific and the destructive, as well as with the beautiful and the beneficent. Yet her fairer forms and gentler influences are undoubtedly the expression of those forces and conditions that go hand in hand with the things that make for our development and well-being.

Probably not till flowers bloomed and birds sang was the earth ripe for man. Not till the bow appeared on the retreating storm-cloud was anything like human life possible. Of savage, elemental Nature, black in tempest and earthquake, hideous in war and pestilence, our poets and nature-students make little, while devout souls seem to experience a cosmic chill when they think of these things.

The majority of persons, I fancy, when they consider seriously the problem, look upon Nature as a sort of connecting link between man and some higher power, neither wholly good nor wholly bad; divine in some aspects, diabolical in others; ministering to our bodies, but hampering and obstructing our souls. They see her a goddess one hour, and a fury the next; destroying life as freely as she gives it; arming one form to devour another; crushing or destroying the fairest as soon as the ugliest; limited in her scope and powers, and not complete in herself, but demanding the existence of something above and beyond herself.

Under the influence of Christianity man has

taken himself out of the category of natural things, both in his origin and in his destiny. Such a gulf separates him from all other creatures, and his mastery over them is so complete that he looks upon himself as exceptional, and as belonging to another order. Nature is only his stepmother, and treats him with the harshness and indifference that often characterize that relation.

When Wordsworth declared himself a worshiper of Nature, was he thinking of Nature as a whole, or only of an abridged and expurgated Nature — Nature in her milder and more beneficent aspects? Was it not the Westmoreland Nature of which he was a worshiper? — a sweet rural Nature, with grassy fells and murmuring streams and bird-haunted solitudes? What would have been his emotion in the desert, in the arctic snows, or in the pestilential forests and jungles of the tropics? Very likely, just what the emotion of most of us would be — a feeling that here are the savage and forbidding and hostile aspects of Nature against which we need to be on our guard. That creative eye and ear to which Wordsworth refers is what mainly distinguishes the attitude of the modern poet toward Nature from the ancient. Sympathy is always creative — "thanks to the human heart by which we live."

The Wordsworthian Nature was of the subjective order; he found it in his own heart, in his dreams by his own fireside, in moments of soul dilation on his

Westmoreland hills, when the meanest flowers that blow could bring to him "thoughts that do often lie too deep for tears."

The Nature that to Wordsworth never betrays us, and to Milton was "wise and frugal," is a humanized, man-made Nature. The Nature we know and wrest our living from, and try to drive sharp bargains with, is of quite a different order. It is no more constant than inconstant, no more wise and frugal than foolish and dissipated; it is not human at all, but unhuman.

When we infuse into it our own idealism, or re-create it in our own image, then we have the Nature of the poets, the Nature that consciously ministers to us and makes the world beautiful for our sake.

When in his first book, "Nature," Emerson says that the aspect of Nature is devout, like the figure of Jesus when he stands with bended head and hands folded upon the breast, we see what a subjective and humanized Nature, a Nature of his own creation, he is considering. His book is not an interpretation of Nature, but an interpretation of his own soul. It is not Nature which stands in an attitude of devotion with bowed head, but Emerson's own spirit in the presence of Nature, or of what he reads into Nature. Yet the Emerson soul is a part of Nature — a peculiar manifestation of its qualities and possibilities, developed through centuries of the interaction of man upon man, through culture, books, religion, meditation.

"The ruin or the blank that we see when we look at Nature," he says, "is in our own eye." Is it not equally true that the harmony and perfection that we see are in our own eye also? In fact, are not all the qualities and attributes which we ascribe to Nature equally the creation of our own minds? The beauty, the sublimity, the power of Nature are experiences of the beholder. The drudge in the fields does not experience them, but the poet, the thinker, the seer, does. Nature becomes very real to us when we come to deal with her practically, when we seek her for specific ends, when we go to her to get our living. But when we go to her in the spirit of disinterested science, the desert, the volcano, the path of the cyclone, are full of the same old meanings, the playground of the same old elements and forces. Nature is what we make her. In his Journal Emerson for a moment sees Nature as she is: "Nature is a swamp, on whose purlieus we see prismatic dewdrops, but her interiors are terrific."

Man is the only creature that turns upon Nature and judges her; he turns upon his own body and mind and judges them; he judges the work of his own hands; he is critical toward all things that surround him; he brings this faculty of judgment into the world.

Emerson refers to "the great Nature in which we

rest as the earth lies in the soft arms of the atmosphere." The earth lies in the soft arms of the atmosphere in the same sense that it lies in the soft arms of its own grasses and flowers; the atmosphere is an appendage of the earth. If the earth literally lies in anything, it is in the soft arms of the all-pervasive ether. Emerson's statement is the inevitable poetizing of Nature in which we all indulge. We make soft arms for our thoughts to lie in, and peaceful paths for our feet to walk in, whatever the literal truth may be. This is the way of art, of poetry, of religion. The way of science and of practical life is a different way. The soft arms become hard with purpose, and rest and contemplation give place to intense activity. I would not have the poet change his way; Nature as reflected in his mind soothes and charms us; it takes on hues from that light which never was on sea or land. But we cannot dispense with the way of science, which makes paths and highways for us through the wilderness of impersonal laws and forces that surge and roar around us. One gives us beauty and one gives us power; one brings a weapon to the hand, the other brings solace to the spirit.

When Bryant identifies God with tempests and thunderbolts, with "whirlwinds that uproot the woods and drown the villages," or with the tidal wave that overwhelms the cities, "with the wrath of the mad, unchained elements" — "tremendous tokens of thy power" — does he make God more lovable or desirable? Well may he say, "From these sterner aspects of thy face, spare me and mine." By way of contrast let me recall that when an earthquake shook California, John Muir cheered himself and friends by saying it was only Mother Earth trotting her children fondly upon her knee! If we identify God with all of Nature, this wrathful Hebrew Jehovah of Bryant is a legitimate conception. There are times when the aerial forces behave like a raving maniac bent upon the destruction of the world — the insensate powers run amuck upon all living things. This is not the God we habitually love and worship, but it is a God from whom there is no escape. As the result of the inevitable action of the natural irrational or unrational forces, tempests and earthquakes and tidal waves do not disturb us; but as the will and purpose of an Almighty Being, Creator of heaven and earth, they give all pious souls a fearful shake-up. We take refuge in such phrases as "the inscrutable ways of God," or "the mysteries of Providence," a Providence whose ways are assuredly "past finding out."

Our State Commissioner of Education, Dr. Finley, in an agricultural address on "Potatoes and Boys," showed God coöperating with the farmer in a way that amused me. "The Almighty," the Commissioner said, "can make, unaided of man, potatoes, but only small potatoes, and of acrid taste. He had to make a primitive man and even teach him to use a hoe, before He, the Omnipotent One, could grow a patch of potatoes." The wild potato, he implied, like the wild grape, the wild apple, the wild melon, was the work of God before he had man to help him; now, with man's help, we have all the improved varieties of potatoes and fruits. We have heard a good deal about the coöperation of man with God, and as a concrete example this potato-growing partnership is very interesting. How far from our habitual attitude of mind is the thought that the Higher Powers concern themselves about our potatoes or our turnips or our pumpkin crop, or have any part or lot in it! Emerson in his Journal expresses another view: "One would think that God made fig-trees and dates, grapes and olives, but the Devil made Baldwin apples and pound pears, cherries and whortle berries, Indian corn and Irish potatoes."

Sir Thomas Browne called Nature the art of God. Viewed in this light we get a new conception of Nature, the artistic conception. We do not ask: Is it good or bad, for us or against us? we are intent on its symbolical or ideal character. Through it God expresses himself as the artist does, be he painter, poet, or musician, through his work, blending the various elements — the light and shade, the good and the bad, the positive and the negative — into a vital, harmonious whole. Creation becomes a picture, or a drama, or a symphony, in which all life plays its part, in which all scenes and conditions, all elemental processes and displays, play their part and unite to make a vast artistic whole. The contradictions in life, the high lights, the deep shadows, the imperfections, the neutral spaces, are but the devices of the artist to enhance the total effect of his work. In ethics and religion we ask of a thing: "Is it good?" In philosophy: "Is it true?" In science: "Is it a fact, and verifiable?" But in art we ask: "Is it beautiful?" or "Is it a real creation?" "Is it one with the vital and flowing currents of the world?"

The artist alone is the creator among men; he is disinterested; he has no purpose but to rival Nature; he subordinates the parts to the whole; he illustrates the divine law of indirections. The bald, literal truth is not for him, but the illusive, the suggestive, the ideal truth. He does not ask what life or Nature are for, or are they good or bad, but he interprets them in terms of the relation of their parts, he reads them in the light of his own soul. He knows there is no picture without shadows, no music without discords, no growth without decay. The artist has "no axe to grind"; to him all is right with the world, however out of joint it may be in our self-seeking lives. Art is synthetic, and puts a soul under the ribs of Death. Science is a straight line, but Art is symbolized by the curve.

To regard Nature, therefore, as the art of God, is to see it complete in itself; all the disharmonies vanish, all our perplexing problems are solved. The earth and the heavens are not for our private good alone, but for all other things. Opposites are blended. Good and bad are relative; heaven and hell are light and shade in the same picture. Our happiness or our misery are secondary; they are the pigments on the painter's palette. The beauty of Nature is its harmony with our constitution; its terror emphasizes our weakness.

Where does the great artist get his laws of art but from his insight into the spirit and method of Nature? They are reflected in his own heart; the act of creation repeats itself in his own handiwork. The true artist has no secondary aims — not to teach or to preach, nor to praise nor condemn; but to portray, and to show us, through the particular, the road to the universal.

Eckermann reports Goethe as saying to him that "Nature's intentions are always good"; but if questioned, Goethe would hardly have maintained that the clouds, the winds, the streams, the tides, gravity, cohesion, and so on, have intentions of any sort, much less intentions directed to us or away from us. Even the wisest among us thus make man the aim and object of Nature. We impose our own psychology upon the very rock and trees.

Goethe always read into Nature his own human

traits; always when he speaks of her he speaks as an artist and poet. He says to Eckermann that Nature "is always true, always serious, always severe; she is always right, and the errors and faults are always those of man. The man who is incapable of appreciating her, she despises; and only to the apt, the pure, the true, does she resign herself and reveal her secrets. The understanding will not reach her; man must be capable of elevating himself to the highest Reason to come into that contact with the Divinity which manifests in the primitive phenomena which dwell behind them and from which they proceed. The divinity works in the living, not in the dead; in the becoming and changing, not in the become and the fixed. Therefore, reason, with its tendency toward the divine, has only to do with the becoming, the living; but understanding has to do with the become, the already fixed, that it may make use of it." In this last we see the germ of Bergson's philosophy. The divinity that dwells behind phenomena, and from which they proceed, is the attempt of the human mind to find the end of that which has no end, the law of causation.

III

EACH FOR ITS OWN SAKE

"Proud man exclaims, 'See all things for my use!'
'See all for mine,' replies the pampered goose."

AND the pampered goose was right: all things are just as much for her use as for man's, while there are reasonable doubts whether things were created for the especial use of either.

Man, like the goose, appropriates what suits him, but is slow to realize the fact that what suits him, or is fitted to his use, depends upon his own powers of adaptation. We can say that he suits it, rather than that it suits him. He has lungs because there is air, and eyes because there are certain vibrations in the ether. In short, nature is the primary fact, and the forms and organs of life the secondary fact.

Goethe said to Eckermann that he followed Kant in looking upon each creature as existing for its own sake. He could not believe, he said, that the cork-trees grow merely that we might stop our bottles, and, he might have added, that rubber-trees grow that we might have rubber overshoes. The lady in a public audience who once asked me what flies are for, evidently thought that God had made a mistake in creating that which annoyed her. I was pleased with a remark of John Muir's in his Sierra book about the poison ivy: "Like most other things not apparently useful to man," he says, "it has few friends, and the blind question, 'Why was it made?' goes on and on with never a guess that first of all it might have been made for itself." Coming from the mouth of a Scotch Presbyterian, this is heretical doctrine. Muir had evidently forgotten his early training.

It is possible for man to make use of poison ivy; in fact it is used in medicine; but who shall dare to say that it was made for that? Flies and poison ivy and all other noxious and harmful things are each and all for their own sakes. They were not made in the sense that we make things. They have come to be what we now find them through the action and interaction of a thousand complex influences. Each has found its place in the scheme of living things, and each acts directly or indirectly upon other forms — is of use to them, or the reverse. Ten thousand things are of use to man, and as many more of no use to him, but to measure all things by his standard of utility is childish, or to ask what mosquitoes and rattlesnakes are for, with an implied impeachment of Nature if they are not of service to man, is an idle question. The water and the air are indispensable to life, but these things are older than life. Life is adapted to them, and not they to it.

The body is full of fluids because earth and air are full of water. From our standpoint man is at the head of animate nature, but the rest of creation is no more exclusively for him than for the least of living things. The good of the world is for whatever or whoever can use it. Houseflies are undoubtedly the enemy of the human race; so are mosquitoes, so are venomous snakes, so are many forms of bacteria, and a thousand other things. (Our egotism prompts us to ask, "Why is evil in the world, anyhow?" But our evil may be the good of some other creature. Our defeat means the triumph of our enemy. It is through this conflict of good and evil, or of things that are for us with things that are against us, that species are developed and perpetuated.)

What kind of a world would it be without what we call evil, without hindrances? To the farmer drought, flood, tornadoes, untimely frosts are evils which he thinks he could well dispense with, but so far as they make a greater struggle necessary, so far as they lead to more self-denial, greater forethought, and so on, they are good in disguise. Hardy, virile characters, like tough timber, in oaks, are developed by unfriendly and opposing forces. Intemperance, greed, cheating, lying, war, are evils in the social and business world; but they teach us the value of their opposites. We react from them. It is a child's question to ask, for example, "Would the world not have been better had there never been any war?" because, since mankind is what it is, wars are inevitable. The absence of wars, as of intemperance, greed, cheating, implies a different mankind, and a different mankind implies a different system of things.

The problem of evil is the problem of life; no evil, no life. The world is thus made. Nature is not half good and half bad; she is wholly good, or wholly bad, according to our relation to her. Fire and flood are bad when they master us, and good when we master and control them. Great good has come out of war, and great evil. The evil always tends to drop out or be obliterated, as the path of cyclones and earthquakes tend to be overgrown and forgotten. Burned cities often rise from their ashes to new life. The effects of evil are finally obliterated; malignant forces have their day, benignant forces go on forever. The world of life, let me repeat, would not be here were not the balance of the account of good and evil on the side of the good, or if good did not come out of evil.

Life is recuperative; if it falls down, it picks itself up again. If a state is devastated by war, in time the cities and towns are rebuilt, and the ranks of peace and industry refilled, though the growth and civilization of that country may have had a terrible setback, and the whole progress of the race be retarded. Evil perishes. The terrible World War, set going by Germany, has depleted the wealth, the life, the well-being of the whole European world, but as the scars it made upon the landscape will in time be effaced, so its effect upon the life of the states and communities will fade and be a memory only. Still the evils it entailed are none the less deplorable. Its heritage of hate, of devastated homes, of depleted treasures, will long continue.

Life, then, in all its forms is for its own sake. It is an end in itself. Many things are inimical to us, and we are equally inimical to many things. We lay the whole of Nature under contribution so far as we can, and we curb and defeat her hostile forces so far as we can, but the world was no more made for man than it was made for mice and midges. When we see how irrespective of us the natural forces go their way, that we can ride them and guide them only as we do wild horses — by being quicker and more masterful than they are — when we know that they will tread us down with the same indifference that we tread down the grass and the weeds, the facts should temper and modify our egotism. When we look into the depths of merely our own solar system, and see vast globes like Jupiter and Saturn, so much older and greater than our little earth, and not yet the abode of any form of life, and probably not within millions of years of such a state, how casual and insignificant man seems! How far from being the end and object of creation!

Doubtless there are numberless worlds and whole systems of worlds in the depths of sidereal space upon which life has never appeared, and numberless other worlds and systems upon which it has had its day and gone out forever. Life is but an incident in the total scheme of things.

To ask what this or that is for, with reference to ourselves, and to conclude that some one or something has blundered if it is not of positive use to us, is, let me repeat, to see and to think as a child. We know what the hooks on the burdock and the stick-seed are for, and what the wings on the maple and the ash-seed are for, but do we know what the stings on the nettle, or the spines on the blackberry or on the thorn-apple tree are for? The cattle eat the nettle, the birds eat the berries, and the wild creatures eat the thorn-apple. How could their seeds get sown if the prickles and thorns defended them against wild life? Spines and thorns seem expressive of moods or conditions in Nature, and to be quite independent of use, as we understand the term.

Nature's ways are so unlike our ways! Her system of economics would soon bring us to bankruptcy. She has no rival, no competitor, no single end in view, no more need to store up wealth than to scatter it. One form gains what another form loses. Humanly speaking, she is always trying to defeat herself. The potato-bug, if left alone, would exterminate the potato and so exterminate itself; the currant-worm would exterminate the currant; the forest worms would exterminate the forests, did not parasites appear and check these ravages. Nature trumps her own trick; she scuttles her own ship; she mines her own defenses; she poisons her own fountains; she sows tares in her own wheat; and yet she wins, because she is the All. The tares are hers, the parasites are hers, the devastating storms and floods are hers, the earthquakes and volcanoes are hers, disease and death are hers, as well as youth and health. The cancer that eats into a man's vitals — what keeps it going but Nature's forces and fluids? The bacteria that flourish in our bodies and bring the scourges of typhoid fever, diphtheria, tuberculosis, are all hers, and a part of her system of things. A malignant tumor is as much an expression of Providence as is a baby or a flower. Nature cuts the ground from under her own feet; she saws off the limb upon which she is perched, but if she falls, she alights in her own lap.

In walking through a blighted potato-field this morning, I said, "Here is one form of vegetable life destroying another form and bringing loss and discontent to the farmer's heart." What purpose in the economy of Nature is served by this blight? Who or what is the gainer? After the minute organisms that prey upon the potato-vines have done their work, they too perish, so that two forms of life are blotted out. What was it all for? Why is this tragedy of one form of life bringing to naught other forms, which we witness on every hand, in vegetable and animal life, and in human history, being constantly enacted? The question, put in this way, is a purely human one; it is applying to the vast scheme of creation purely human standards. We instinctively ask the why and the wherefore of things, and in our practical lives try to avoid letting one hand defeat the other as Nature does in the above incident. We guard one form of life against another hostile form. Our aim is to make things pull together for our own advantage. We seek to check the ravages of the tent caterpillar, the forest worms, the gypsy moth, the potato-beetle, and the invisible enemies that rot our grapes and mar our apples, as well as the germs that sow fatal diseases in our midst. But not so Nature. She does not take sides. As I have said, she has no special and limited aims. The stakes are hers, whoever wins. One condition of the season favors the growth of the potato-vines; another condition favors the development of the fungus that destroys them. Nature is just as much on the side of the rat as on the side of the cat; she arms each to defeat the other, and the fittest survives. She has not given the rabbit strength or ferocity, but she has given her speed and a sleepless eye and great fecundity, and her enemies do not cut her off.

The struggle and competition of life go on everywhere. But life is not all a struggle; it is unity and coöperation as well. The trees of the forest protect one another; one form of life profits by another form.

In the whole drama of organic nature we find waste and prodigality. Our economics are set at naught by the power that works to no special ends, but to all ends, and finds its account in the tumor that eats up the man, as much as in the man himself, in the fungi that destroy the potato crop, or the chestnut-trees, as truly as in these things themselves. Yet behold what specialization and what development has taken place in spite of these cross-purposes, this chaos of conflicting interests! Out of discord has come harmony; out of conflict has come peace; out of death has come life; out of the reptile has come the bird; out of the beast has come man; out of the savage has come the moral conscience; out of the tribe has come the nation; out of tyranny has come democracy. It is the waste, the delays, the pain, the price to be paid, that appall us.

We must regard creation as a whole, as the evolution of worlds and systems, and not concentrate our attention upon man and his ways, or upon the earth — so small a part of our solar system.

Our benevolent institutions are not types of the universe; our idea of fatherhood does not fit the Eternal.

Our fathers had a complete and consistent explanation of the problem of evil that so perplexes us. They invented or postulated two opposing and contending principles in the world — one divine, the other diabolical. One they named God, the other,

Satan. Their conception of God would not allow them to saddle all the evil and misery of the world upon him; they had to look for a scapegoat, and they found him in the Devil. One is just as necessary to a consistent cosmogony as the other. If we must have an all-wise, all-merciful, all-powerful, all-loving God — the author of all good and the contemner of all evil — we must also have a god of the opposite type, the great mischief-maker and enemy of human happiness — the author of war, pestilence, famine, disease, and of all that hinders and defeats the reign of the perfect good. Without the conception of the Devil, we are forced to the conclusion, either that God is not omnipotent, or that he is responsible for all the sin and suffering in the world. If you make man this Devil, then who made man?

Wrestle with the problem as we may, we are impaled on one or the other horn of the dilemma. Our traditional God is more cruel and more indifferent to human suffering than any tyrant that ever gloated over human blood and agony, or else he is fearfully limited in his power for good.

With a Devil at our disposal to whom we can impute the evils of life, the situation clears up, and God emerges, shorn of his omnipotence, it is true, but still the symbol of goodness and love.

In our day the Devil has lost his prestige and is much discredited. As a power in men's minds his

reign is over, and hell, his headquarters, no longer
casts its lurid light upon human life.

In an equal measure the old Hebraic conception
of God as a much-magnified man, the king and
ruler of heaven and earth, with heaven as his throne,
has gone out. God is now little more than a name
for that tendency or power in the universe which
makes for righteousness, and which has brought
evolution thus far on its course.

To account for the world as we find it, we are
compelled to look upon it as the inevitable result
of the clashing and interaction of purely natural
forces resulting in both so-called good and evil; that
is, in what is favorable to life, and in what is against
life. But as life is adaptive and assimilative, it slowly
turns the evil into good, of course at the expense of
delays and waste and suffering, and thus development becomes possible, and man, after untold millions of years, appears.

When we look forth upon the universe, what do
we see? When we look upon the non-living world,
we see a mere welter and chaos of material forces —
a conflict of chemical and physical principles seeking a stable equilibrium — water running, winds
blowing, mountains decaying, stars and systems
whirling, suns waning or waxing, nebulæ condens-
ing, vast orbs colliding, and all issuing in a certain
order and system under the rule of purely mechanical and mathematical laws. The stellar universe is a

vast machine, amenable to the measurements and calculations of the astronomers. The eclipses all occur exactly on time, and the planets revolve in their orbits without the untruth, as Whitman says, of a single second. The disorder and disruptions which occur are inside of vast fundamental laws. Our mountains and seas are shaken by earthquakes, and the earth's surface is swept by cyclones and the seashores are devastated by tidal waves, yet these things are only phases of the effort toward a fixed equilibrium. The earth's surface as we now behold it, the distribution of land and water, of mountain and plain, the procession of the seasons, our whole weather system, the friendly and the unfriendly forces, are all the outcome of this clash and stress of the physical forces, which make a paradise of some places and the opposite of others.

When we look upon the living world as revealed in the geologic record, we still see a kind of welter and chaos, but we also see the advent of new principles not entirely subject to mechanical and mathematical laws. Life goes its way and takes liberties with its physical environment. Living bodies change and develop as the non-living do not. The various organic forms "rise on stepping-stones of their dead selves," and incalculably slow transformations of lower forms into higher take place, but not without appalling delays and waste and suffering. Chemical and mechanical laws are still in full force, but they

appear to be in the service of a new principle; an
organizing tendency of a new kind is at work in the
world; chance and necessity seem to play a less conspicuous part. Yet there is nothing that meets our
idea of justice, or mercy, or economy of effort.

For millions upon millions of years the earth
swarmed with low, all but brainless creatures. The
monsters of sea and land that appeared in the middle period were huge and terrible in body and limb,
but very small in capacity of brain. Huge ganglions,
or knots of nervous tissue, in different parts of their
bodies seem to have served as a substitute for a cen-
tralized brain and a complex nervous system. The
brontosaurus, seventy feet long, with a body weighing many tons, had a head not much larger than a
man's double fists. Brains as yet played a very subordinate part in the world. Reptiles and half-reptiles
possessed the earth. The age of mammals was as yet
only hinted at. But after long geologic ages, mammals came to the front, holding the precious possi-
bility of man, and reptiles were relegated to the rear.
The animal brain increased, wit began to get the
better of brute force, and the small and feeble ancestors of man appeared in the biological drama. They
were like small and timid supernumeraries skulk-
ing or hiding on the wings of the stage. Lemurs and
monkeys appeared long before there were any signs
of the anthropoid apes, and the anthropoid apes were
in evidence long before the first rude man appeared.

In all the vast stretch of geologic and biologic time, do we see any evidence of the active existence of the God and the Devil of our fathers? Not unless we identify them with the material forces that then ruled and shaped the world, and these forces, by any other name, are of the same impersonal, impartial, unforgiving character as is disclosed in our dealings with them to-day.

When we turn to the higher forms of organic life, especially to man and his history, what do we see? We still behold the same trial-and-error method, the same cruelty, waste, delays, and suffering that we behold in the lower forms. We see progress, we see the growth of ethical principles, we see man's increasing mastery over the forces of nature and over himself, but in the competition of races and nations, the race is still to the swift and the battle to the strong. We see a high standard of individual morality contending with a low standard of international morality. We still see civilized nations looking upon treaties as "scraps of paper"; we see them regarding their neighbors as rivals and enemies; we see millions of men that have not the shadow of a grievance against one another, fiercely trying to slay one another, and praying to the same God for victory. We see the nefarious doctrine that physical might makes moral right written in lines of blood and fire across the face of whole kingdoms; we see the legitimate competitions of peace and industry turned into the strife of armed conquest; we see a small and peaceful nation trampled underfoot by a big nation bent upon plunder and conquest; we see hatred toward a kindred nation glorified, and the murder of innocent women and children and other non-combatants adopted as a fixed policy; in fact, we see all the vast resources of science and of modern civilization wedded to the spirit of the Hun, and turned loose in a war for world-dominion. The results of eighteen centuries of Christian culture come off the German nation like a whitewash in this craze and fury of the military spirit; the German people stand revealed as at heart unmitigated barbarians, wonderfully efficient, but wonderfully inhuman. If we appeal to the supernatural to account for things, we certainly need a Devil, if not several of them, to account for the temper of the German mind during the late war. No wonder the good people are losing faith, and are shocked and dismayed at the thought that their all-loving, omnipotent God permits these things.

Down the whole course of history we see no other powers at work than those that are about us. Good is in the ascendancy everywhere, or soon will be; evil dies out; the wicked cease from troubling; the amelioration of mankind goes on; and no God or Devil hinders or favors.

Nature is both God and Devil, and natural law is supreme in the world. The moral consciousness of man, — all our dreams of perfection, of immortality, of the good, the beautiful, the true, all our veneration and our religious aspirations, — this is Nature, too.

Man is a part of the universe; all that we call good in him, and all that we call bad, are a part of the universe. The God he worships is his own shadow cast upon the heavens, and the Devil he fears is his own shadow likewise. The divine is the human, magnified and exalted; the satanic is the human, magnified and debased.

We find God in Nature by projecting ourselves there; we find him in the course of history by reading our own ideals into human events; we find him in our daily lives by listening to the whisperings of our own inherited and acquired consciences, and by dwelling upon the fatality that rules our lives.

We had nothing to do with our appearance here in this world, or with the form our bodies take, or with our temperaments, and, only in a degree, with our dispositions. Some power other than ourselves brought us here and maintains us here for a period, as it brought here and maintains all other forms of life; but, I repeat, that power is inseparable from the physical and chemical forces, and goes its way whether we prosper or perish. Yet it is more positive than negative, more for us than against us, else we should not be here.

Where does man get his ethical standards? Where

does he get his eyes, his ears, his heart? He gets them where he got his life — from natural sources. He gets them whence he got his sense of art, of beauty, of harmony. There are no moral standards in Nature apart from man, but as man is a part of Nature, so are these, and all other standards. So are all religions, arts, literatures, philosophies, heroisms, self-denials, as well as all idolatries, superstitions, sorceries, cruelties, wrongs, failures, a part of Nature.

Is the big-brained man of to-day any less a part of Nature than the low-browed, long-jawed man of Pliocene times?

The humanization of God leads us into many difficulties. If He is a personal being with attributes and emotions like our own, then we are forced to the conclusion that He is no better than we are — that He has our faults as well as our virtues, our cruelty as well as our love. He is a party to all the wrongs and crimes and suffering that darken the earth; He permits wars and pestilence and famine and earthquakes and tornadoes, and all the consuming and agonizing diseases that flesh is heir to. He is an infinite man with infinite powers for good and evil.

In the long drama of animal evolution there has evidently been as much suffering as pleasure, and of the drama of human history the same may be said: pain, failure, delay, injustice, to all of which our humanized God has been a party. No wonder our fathers struggled over the problem of the ways of God to man. As soon as they put themselves in his place, they felt the need of some grounds upon which to justify his dealings with the beings He had created. But they searched, and their descendants still search, in vain. If we see God as a man, no matter how mighty, He is still guilty of what few finite men would be guilty. What men would be guilty of permitting the sin and misery that fill the world at this, or any other, time?

The Nature God neither sends calamities nor wills them — they are an inevitable part of the growth and development of things; they are eddies in the stream of forces. What we call evil is evil only from our point of view; evil is a human word and not the word of the Infinite. If the world were something made by a Maker external to it, then it were pertinent to ask, Why not make it a better world? Why not leave out pain and sin and all other phases of evil? But the world is not something made, and it did not have a Maker, ás we use those words. The universe *is*, and always has been, "from everlasting to everlasting," and man is a part of it, and his life is subject to the same vicissitudes as the rest of creation. Man has come into this sense of right and wrong, of justice and mercy, of truth and falsehood, of good and evil, as necessary conditions of his development, but those things are not absolute; they pertain to him alone. The physical forces break out of their natural bounds and run riot for a season; the human forces do the same thing and give rise to various excesses. The crimes and misdemeanors of man are exceptional as the outbreaks in nature are exceptional. They relate man to nature and show how the same plan runs through both. A world with storm and the warring and violence of the elements left out would be a radically different world — an impossible world. And a world of man, a Quaker world, is equally impossible.

If some being of infinite wisdom and love had made the world and made man to live in it, we could ask him some embarrassing questions; but, let me repeat, the world was not made, it is only a link in a chain of cosmic events, and it is not for man any more than for any other creature. Each must "work out his own salvation, with fear and trembling."

Introduce design into nature and you humanize it and get into difficulties at once. It is above design. We have no language in which to speak the ultimate truth, no language in which to describe the character and the doings of the Infinite. The ways of the Infinite are not only past finding out, they are unspeakable by reason of our finite relations to them. We cannot arraign the Nature God. It does not design, nor make, nor govern, nor employ means to ends, as do the man-made gods. It *is.* All things are a part of its infinite complexity. Nature rests forever in itself. It neither fails nor succeeds. In itself it is neither good nor evil, neither divine nor devilish; it is all things to all men, because they are all things to it. It is neither one nor many; it is the Infinite. In these vain attempts to define or describe the indefinable I have no language but that of the finite, no language but that of our limited or circumscribed relation to the world of concrete and fragmentary things. Hence I am constantly like the plains ranger caught by his own lasso, or the angler caught by his own hook.

Emerson said that in trying to define the Eternal we need a language that differs from our everyday speech as much as algebra differs from arithmetic. Outside of the physical organism there is neither pleasure nor pain, good nor bad, light nor dark, sound nor silence, heat nor cold, big nor little, hard nor soft ; all these things are but words in which we describe our sensations. When there is no ear, there is no sound, but only motion in the air; when there is no eye, there is no light or color, but only motion in the ether; when there are no nerves, there is no heat or cold, but only motion, more or less, in the molecules of matter. Degrees and differences belong to the region of our finite minds. In trying to define or state the Infinite, we are off the sphere, outside the realm of experience, and our words have no meaning.

It is the circular or orbicular character of creation that baffles us. We cannot fit the sphere into the triangles and parallelograms of the terms of our experience. We cannot square the circle of Infinity. The terms "love," "anger," "mercy," "fatherhood," do not apply to God any more than "over" or "under," or "beginning" or "end," apply to the sphere. In regard to God, the language of science and mathematics is one with the language of worship and ecstasy.

I find I have never been burdened by a sense of my duty to God. My duty to my fellow-men and to myself is plain enough, but the word is not adequate to express any relation I may hold to the Eternal. Do I owe any duty to gravity without which I could not move or lift my hand, or any duty to the sunshine or to the rains and the winds? Instinctively, unconsciously, for the most part we obey the law of gravity, and instinctively we adjust ourselves to all the natural forces, not from a sense of duty, but from a sense of self-preservation. These things are a part of our lives and not something to which we hold only a casual and precarious or external relation. My relation to the Eternal is not that of an inferior to a superior, or of a beneficiary to his benefactor, or of a subject to his king. It is that of the leaf to the branch, of the fruit to the tree, of the babe in the womb to its mother. It is a vital and an inevitable relation. It cannot be broken. It is not a matter of will or choice. We are embosomed in the Eternal Beneficence, whether we desire it or not.

EACH FOR ITS OWN SAKE

Those good persons who go through life looking upon the Eternal as a power external to themselves, saluting him as the soldier salutes his officer, are not as truly religious as they think they are. The old conception of an external God, the supreme ruler of the universe, with whom Moses talked and walked and even saw the hinder parts of, is out of date in our time. Still the overarching thought of the Infinite and the Eternal, in whom we live and move and have our being, must at times awaken in the minds of all of us, and lend dignity and sobriety to our lives.

But the other world fades as this world brightens. Science has made this world so interesting and wonderful, and our minds find such scope in it for the exercise of all their powers, that thoughts of another world are becoming foreign to us. We shall never exhaust the beauties and the wonders and the possibilities of this. To feel at home on this planet, and that it is, with all its drawbacks, the best possible world, I look upon as the supreme felicity of life.

When we look at it in its mere physical and chemical aspects, its play of forces, tangible and intangible, its reservoir of energy, its "journeying of atoms," its radiating electrons, its magnetic currents, its transmutations and cycles of change, its hidden but potent activities, its streaming auroras, its changing seasons, its myriad forms of life, and a thousand other things — all make it a unique and most desirable habitation.

When we consider it in its astronomical aspects as a celestial body floating in the luminiferous ether as in a sea, held in leash by the sun, and as sensitive to its changes as the poplar leaf to the wind, vast beyond our power to visualize, yet only a grain of sand on the shores of the Infinite, an evening or a morning star to the beings on other planets, if there are such, mottled with shining seas or green and white continents and canopied with many-hued cloud draperies, and existing in closest intimacies with the wonders and the potencies of the sidereal heavens — a veritable fruit on the vast sidereal tree of life — when we realize all this, and more, can we conceive of a more desirable or a better-founded and better-furnished world? The voyage we make upon it may be a long one; if we claim the century of life which Nature seems to have allotted us on conditions, we shall travel about thirty-six billions of miles in our annual voyages around the sun, and how many more millions with the sun around his sun, we know not. A world made of the common stuff of the universe, a handful of the dust of the cosmos, yet thrilling with life, producing the race of man, evolving the brain of Plato, of Aristotle, of Bacon, the soul of Emerson, of Whitman, the heart of Christ — a heavenly abode surely. Let us try to make amends for depreciating it, for spurning it, for surrendering it to the Devil, and for turning from it in search of a better.

Our religion is at fault, our saints have betrayed us, our theologians have blackened and defaced our earthly temple, and swapped it off for cloud mansions in the Land of Nowhere. The heavens embrace us always; the far-off is here, close at hand; the ground under your door-stone is a part of the morning star. If we could only pull ourselves up out of our absorption in trivial affairs, out of the petty turmoil of our practical lives, and see ourselves and our world in perspective and as a part of the celestial order, we could cease to weep and wail over our prosaic existence.

The astronomic view of our world, and the Darwinian view of our lives must go together. As one came out of the whirling, fiery nebulæ, so the other came out of the struggling, slowly evolving, biological world of the unicellular life of the old seas.

Biologic time sets its seal upon one, and cosmic time upon the other. Dignity and beauty and meaning are given to our lives when we see far enough and wide enough, when we see the forces that minister to us, and the natural order of which we form a part.

IV

THE UNIVERSAL BENEFICENCE

THAT bodies rise in the air does not disprove gravity; on the contrary, it proves it. The pull of gravity never lets go of the bullet from the gun; no matter how high or how far it goes, down it comes, sometime, somewhere.

Without this pull the gun would have no power. There is no force when there is nothing to resist force. The force of the chemical reaction in the gun on the explosion of the powder is hurled back by the weight and resistance of the gun, all the result of gravity, and sends the bullet high or far, but does not for a second break its hold upon it. Smoke rises because the air falls; clouds float because of the greater weight of something beneath them. The river flows because its banks do not.

The goodness of nature is the universal fact, like gravity, and its evils and enmities and hindrances only prove the law.

The waters of the globe seek their level, seek to reach a haven of everlasting repose; but behold how that purpose is forever frustrated, and the currents never cease. It is as if the creeks and rivers never reached the sea; they are traveling that way forever; it is as if the great ocean currents and submarine Amazons and Mississippis were seeking an escape which they never find; their quest is ever renewed. Nature is Nature because her work is never complete; her journey is never ended; the fixity and equilibrium which her elements appear to seek, is ever deferred; life can appear and go on only in a changing, unstable world, and it is this flux and mutability of things that bring all our woe, and all our joy as well. If winds did not blow, and bodies fall, and fire consume, and floods overpower, if the equilibrium of things were not perpetually broken, — which opens the door to all our troubles and disasters, — where should we find the conditions of our life?

Life has appeared in an unstable world, and is conditioned upon this instability. Fixity means death. It is in the line of organic effort that living forms appear; it is in an imperfect world that we strive for the perfection that we never reach. Blessed be the fact that our capacity for life, for happiness, is always greater than the day yields. Satiety checks effort.

The Nature Providence is stern and even cruel in some of its dealings with us, but not in all, else we should run away from home. It is genial and friendly in the genial season — in a June meadow, in a field of ripening grain, in an orchard bending with fruit, in the cattle on a thousand hills, in the shade of the friendly trees, in the bubbling springs, in the paths by the green fields and by still waters, and in ten thousand other aspects of its manifold works. It is not friendly in the tropical jungles, nor amid the snows and blizzards of the polar regions, but upon four fifths of the surface of the globe it may be said to be friendly or neutral. Man is armed to face its hostile aspects and to turn its very wrath to account. If God maketh the wrath of man to praise Him, so man maketh the wrath of God to serve him, as when he subdues and controls Nature's destructive forces, tames the lightning and harnesses Niagara. He has not bound the cyclone yet, nor warmed himself by the volcano, nor moved mountains from his path with the earthquake, but he may do it yet. He is fast drawing the fangs of contagious diseases, thus adding to his length of days.

The Nature Providence working in man and through him has made the world more fit for man's abode.

Action and reaction are the steps by which life ascends. Nature acts upon man and man reacts upon nature. The labor the farmer puts into the soil comes back to him with interest, and enables him to labor more. The capital of life grows in that way; action and reaction; up we go.

"Are God and Nature then at strife?" asks Tennyson, baffled and unsettled by what he sees about him. There is strife in the living world, the struggle of existence. In the non-living, there is collision, disruption, overthrow. The apparent strife between the two worlds is an effort toward adjustment on the part of the living — to master and utilize the non-living. The inorganic goes its way under the leash of physical laws, heedless of the organic. Myriads of living things are crushed and destroyed by the ruthless onward flow of the non-living. There is life in the world because life is plastic and persistent and adaptive, and perpetually escapes from the blind forces that would destroy it — the winds, the floods, the frost, the heat, gravity, earthquakes, chemical reactions, and so on. Every living thing runs the gantlet of the insensate mechanical and chemical forces. But this is not strife in our human sense; it is the discipline of nature. No living thing could begin or continue without these forces which at times are so hostile. Like faithful gardeners preparing the seed-beds, they prepared the earth for the abode of man and all other living forms. They made the soil, they bring the rains, they begat the winds, they prearranged all the conditions of life; but life itself is a mystery, the great mystery, super-mechanical, super-chemical, dependent upon these forces, but not begotten by them. They are its servants.

The struggle in the world of living forms is a condition of development, growing things are made strong by the force of the obstacles they overcome.

From our limited human point of view there are phases of creation that make it look like a game between intelligent contending forces, or as if one god tried to undo the work of another god, or at least to mar and hinder his work — some mischievous and malignant spirit that sows tares amid the wheat, that retards development, that invents parasites, that produces the malformed, that scatters the germs of disease. How much at heart Nature seems to have the production and well-being of offspring, yet what failures there are! in the human realm the deformed, the monstrous, the idiotic. It seems as if all things in heaven and earth had a stake in a perfect baby and in its growth and development. A land swarming with beautiful and happy children should make the very stars rejoice. Motherhood itself is a beautiful and divine symbol, yet what perils attend it! In many cases mother and child sink into the same grave. Then along comes some malignant spirit and sows the germs of infantile paralysis, and great numbers of children perish, and still greater numbers are crippled and deformed for life. What a miscarriage of nature is that! What a calamity, and unmitigated evil!

When an insect stings a leaf or plant-stalk and the plant forthwith builds a cradle and nursery for the young of the insect, that is one form of life using another form; or when a parasitical bird, such as the European cuckoo, or our cowbird, lays its egg in the nest of another bird, that is the same thing — life is still triumphant. But when the germs of a contagious disease — tuberculosis, diphtheria, scarlet fever — invade the human system and finally result in its destruction, then dissolution is triumphant; all this delicately and elaborately organized matter comes to naught. In this we see the failure of the tendency or impulsion in matter which results in organization — the mystery and the miracle of vitality, as Tyndall called it, and the triumph of the contrary impulse or disorganization, unless we regard the destructive and death-dealing germs themselves as a triumph of organization, which, from the scientific point of view, they surely are. Then we have Nature playing one hand against the other. From our point of view it is like pulling down a temple and reducing the bricks and stones to dust for the use of ants. But who shall say that Nature is not just as careful of the ant as of the man? — which is, of course, a distasteful bit of news to the man.

When one thinks of the myriads of minute living organisms that pervade and make up his own body, of their struggles and activities, their antagonisms and coöperations, their victories and defeats, — the cells coöperating and building up the organs, the organs coöperating and building up the body, the phagocytes policing the blood and destroying the invading germs, the intestinal flora contending with

one another for the possession of the soil, the ferments, the enzymes, — when one thinks of all this
and more, and how little aware the man is of all
this strife and effort and activity within him, —
how he himself, body and mind, is the result of it
all, — one has a dim vision of all our strife and effort
in this world as a part of the vital movements of a
vast system of things, or of a Being that is no more
cognizant of our wars and struggles and triumphs
than we are of the histories of the little people that
keep up the functional integrity of our own systems.

Man can himself make short work of the ants
unless he encounters their devouring hosts in a
tropical jungle, in which case they may make
short work of him. He can often slay with his an-
tiseptics the disease germs that are destroying him,
but not always; the balance of nature is often on
their side. Whichever triumphs, Nature wins, because all are parts of her system. The capital invested is hers alone. Man thinks a part of it is
his, because he forgets that he too is a part of
Nature, and that whatever is his, is hers.

How are we to reconcile the obvious facts of
evolution, namely, that throughout the biological
ages there has been an impulse in Nature steadily
working toward the development of man, with the
still more obvious fact that Nature cares no more
for the individual man than she does for the individual of any other species? She will drown him,

starve him, freeze him, crush him, as quickly as she will any other form of life. Is the account balanced by the fact that she has given him the wit and the power to avoid these calamities in a larger measure than she has given them to any other creature? That is the way the great mystery works. Every creature is exposed to the hazards of its kind, but within its reach are always the benefits and advantages of its kind, and these latter have steadily kept in the lead. The evolutionary impulse toward the horse, toward the dog, toward the bird, has apparently been as jealously guarded and promoted as the impulse toward man. Man in his own conceit is at the head of the animal kingdom, and the whole creation is for him, though there are other animals that surpass him in strength, speed, and endurance. But he alone masters and makes servants of the inorganic forces, and thus rules the world below him.

I set out to say that the beneficent force or Providence that brought us here has had to struggle with the non-beneficent in inert matter, and, at times, with what looks like the deliberately malignant in living matter; micro-organisms everywhere lying in wait for tangible bodies and reducing them back to the original dust out of which they came — the work of one god being held up or wrecked by another god. In the vegetable kingdom are blights and scabs and many forms of fungus diseases; in the animal are hostile bacteria and parasites work-

ing without and within. Little wonder our fathers
had to invent a Devil, or a hierarchy of good and
evil spirits contending with one another, to explain
the enigmas of life! But that the good spirits have
prevailed over their enemies, that the Natural
Providence has been on our side, is, as I have
pointed out, proved by the fact that we are actually here, and that life is good to us.

The evil of the world is seen to be ingrained in the
nature of things, and it has been a spur to development. All the great human evils have been dis-
ciplinary. There is always a surplusage, rarely just
enough and no more. The gods of life rarely make a
clean, neat job of it; there are needless pains, needless wastes, needless failures, needless delays. The
good of war — the fortitude, the self-denial, the
heroism — we cannot separate from the evil; the
good of avarice or greed — industry, thrift, foresight — we cannot separate from the evil. The
wealth-gatherers keep the currents going, they sub-
due the wilderness, they reclaim the deserts, they
develop the earth's resources, they extend the
boundaries of civilization, but the evils that follow
in their train are many and great. Yet how are we to
have the one without the other? Disease is also a
kind of trial by battle; it weeds out the weak, the
physically unfit, and hardens and toughens the
race.

The Natural Providence does not study economy,

it is not in business with rivals and competitors; bankruptcy is not one of its dangers, it can always meet its obligations; all the goods and all the gold and silver in the universe belong to it. Its methods are too vast and complex for our ideas of prudence and economy. We cannot deal with the whole, but only with its parts. There are no lines and boundaries to the sphere, and no well-defined cleavage between the good and the evil in nature and in life. The broad margin of needless misery and waste in the life of a man as of a nation is a part of the inexactitude and indifference that pervades the whole of nature. From the point of view of the Natural Providence it does not matter, the result is sure; but from our point of view — victims of cyclones, earthquakes, wars, famines, pestilence as we are — it matters a great deal. The streams and rivers throughout the land are bearers of many blessings; the evils they bring are minor and are soon forgotten.

The whole living world is so interrelated and interdependent, and hinges so completely upon the non-living, that our analysis and interpretation of it must of necessity be very imperfect. But the creative energy works to no specific ends, or rather it works to all ends. As every point on the surface of the globe is equally on the top at all times, so the whole system of living nature balances on any given object. I saw a book of poems recently, called "The

Road to Everywhere" — vague as Nature herself. All her roads are roads to everywhere. They may lead you to your own garden, or to the North Pole, or to the fixed stars, or may end where they began.

Nature is a great traveler, but she never gets away from home; she takes all her possessions along with her, and her course is without direction, and without beginning or end. The most startling contradiction you can make expresses her best. She is the sum of all opposites, the success of all failures, the good of all evil.

When we think we have cut out Nature, we have only substituted another phase; when our balloon mounts in spite of gravity, it is still gravity that makes it mount; when we clear the soil of its natural growth and plant our own crop, Nature is still our gardener; we have only placed other seeds of her own in her hands. When we have improved upon her, we have only prevailed upon her to second our efforts; we get ahead of her by following out the hints she gives us; when we trump her trick, it is with her own cards. When we fancy we assist Nature, as we say that we do with our drugs, it is she who gives the efficiency to the drugs. We may fancy that the sun is in the heavens solely to give light and warmth to the planets, which it surely does, but behold, what a mere fraction of the light and heat of the sun is intercepted by the slender girdle of worlds that surround it! The rays go out

64

equally in all directions, they penetrate all space. The sun, with reference to its light and heat, is at the center of an infinite hollow sphere, and not one millionth part of its rays falls upon the worlds that circle around it. This is typical of Nature's bounty. The thought and solicitude of the creative energy is directed to me and you personally in the same wholesale way. The planets of our system are lighted and warmed as effectually as if the sun shone for them alone, and man is the beneficiary of the heavens as completely as if indeed the whole creation were directed especially to him. Here is another point: the night and darkness in nature are local and limited; the universe is flooded with light; the black shadows themselves are born of the light. Though astronomers tell us that sidereal space is strewn with dead worlds and extinct suns, give time enough and they will all be quickened and rekindled. Light and life are the positive facts in nature, darkness and death the negative.

When we single out man and fix our attention upon him as the sole end of creation, and judge the whole by his partial standards, man —

> "Who trusted God was love indeed
> And love Creation's final law —
> Though Nature, red in tooth and claw
> With ravine, shrieked against his creed" —

when we do this, all is confusion and contradiction. Love *is* "creation's final law," but not the love of the mother for her child, or even of the bird for its young, but the love of the eye for the light, of the flower for the sun, the love of the plants for the rain and the dew, the love of man for his kind, and of the dog for his kind. Attraction, affiliation, assimilation — like unto like is the rule of life.

The organism fits itself to its environment; the Providence in Nature enables it to do so. The light is not fitted to the eye; the light creates the eye; the vibrations in the air create the ear. God, or the Eternal, is love because He brooded man into being, and all other forms of life that support man. He made the heavens and the earth for man's good, by making man a part of them and able to avail himself of their bounty. But when we look forth into the universe, and expect to see something like human care and affection in the operation of the great elemental laws and forces, we are bound to be shocked. It is not there, and well that it is not. A universe run on the principles of human economy, human charity, and partiality would be a failure. It is our human weakness that yearns for this. It is our earthly father that has begotten in us our conception of a heavenly father. But then this very conception and desire is a part of nature — springs from the Eternal, and is in that sense authentic. We cannot separate ourselves from nature, or from the Eternal, any more than we can jump off the planet. It is only the conception of a human or man-made God that men rebel against. Thus comes in the discord that Tennyson sees and feels. He is looking for a human providence in nature. Wisdom, love, mercy, justice, are human attributes. We call them divine, and it is well, but they do not exist outside of man. Man is himself the only God, and he was evolved from nature. The divine and the godlike are therefore in nature; yes, in conjunction with what we call the demoniacal — love twined with enmity, the good a partner with the bad.

"I bring to life, I bring to death;
The spirit does but mean the breath."

Plagues and famines and wars are fortuitous and not a part of the regular order like health, or growth, or development. They are accidents of nature. The cloud-burst that sends the creek out of its banks is an accident in the same sense; it is an exceptional occurrence. If the fountains of nature were not full enough and permanent enough to stand such drains, or if the tendency in nature to a certain order and moderation were less marked, life would disappear from the globe. Nature's capital of life is invested in ten thousand enterprises and the risks are many, but if the gains did not exceed the losses, if more seeds did not fall upon fertile places than upon barren, if more babies did not survive than perish, what would become of us? In our human schemes we aim to cut out losses, waste, delays and failure, and arraign the Eternal when it does not follow the same methods. But so far as I can see all that the Eternal aims at in the vast business of the universe is to keep the capital unimpaired and live on the income. The inroads which storms, pestilence, earthquakes make upon it are soon made good and some interest does accrue. <u>Life does advance.</u>

In the course of the biologic ages there has been a great loss in species, apparently without any loss in the development impulse. New species appear as the old disappear. Nature's investment in mere size and brute strength was doubtless a good one under the conditions, but she gradually changed it and began to lay the emphasis upon size of brain and complexity of nervous system, just as man in his material civilization has passed from the simple to the complex, from the go-cart to the automobile, from the signal fires to telegraph and telephone. The failures and shortcomings of the Eternal, as well as the progress of its work, are analogous to those of man. Indeed, God is no more a god than man is. He evinces the same methods, the same mixture of good and evil, the same progress from the simple to the complex, the same survival of the fittest. We exalt and magnify our little human attributes and name it God; we magnify and intensify our bad traits and call it the Devil. One is as real as the other. Both are real to the imagination of man, but Nature knows them not, except so far as she knows them in and through man.

THE UNIVERSAL BENEFICENCE

On a midsummer day, calm, clear, warm, the leaves shining, the grain and grass ripening, the waters sparkling, the birds singing, we see and feel the beneficence of Nature. How good it all is! What a joy to be alive! If the day were to end in a fury of wind and storm, breaking the trees, unroofing the houses, and destroying the crops, we should be seeing the opposite side of Nature, what we call the malevolent side. Fair days now and then have such endings, but they are the exception; living nature survives them and soon forgets them. Their scars may long remain, but they finally disappear. Total nature is overpoweringly on the side of life. But for all this, when we talk about the fatherhood of God, his loving solicitude, we talk in parables. There is not even the shadow of analogy between the wholesale bounty of Nature and the care and providence of a human father. Striding through the universe goes the Eternal, crushed worlds on one hand and worlds being created on the other; no special act of love or mercy or guidance, but a providence like the rains, the sunshine, the seasons.

When we say hard things about Nature — accuse her of cruelty, of savagery, of indifference — we fall short of our proper filial respect toward her. She is the mother of us all; neither an indulgent mother, nor a cruel stepmother. In many respects the gifts she has lavished upon us only make her own poverty the more conspicuous. Where she got the gift of

reason which she has bestowed upon man, together
with the sense of justice and of mercy, the moral
consciousness, the æsthetic perceptions, the capacity for learning her secrets and mastering her
forces, are puzzling questions. We may say that
man achieved these things himself; but who or
what made him capable of achieving them, what
made him man, and out of the same elements that
his dog or his horse is made?

Nature does not reason; she has no moral consciousness; she does not economize her resources;
she is not efficient, she is wasteful and dilatory, and
spends with one hand what she saves with the other.
She is blind; her method is the hit-and-miss method
of a man who fights in the dark. She hits her mark,
not because she aims at it, but because she shoots in
all directions. She fills the air with her bullets. She
wants to plant in yonder marsh her cat-tail flag, or
her purple loosestrife, and she trusts her seeds to
every wind that blows, and to the foot of every
bird that visits her marshes, no matter which way
they are going. And in time her marsh gets planted.
The pollen from her trees and plants drifts in clouds
in order that one minute grain of it may find the
pistil that is waiting for it somewhere in the next
wood or field. She trusts her nuts to every vagabond jay or crow or squirrel that comes along, in
hopes that some of them will be dropped or hidden
and thus get planted. She trims her trees, and thins

her forests, or reforests her lands, in the most roundabout, dilatory, and inefficient manner. No plan, no system, no economy of effort or of material; and yet she "gets there," because she is not limited as to time or resources. She is in business with unlimited capital and unlimited opportunities; she has no competitors; her stockholders are all of one mind, and all roads lead to her markets. The winds, the streams, the rains, the snows, fire, flood, tornado, earthquake, are all her servitors. She does not stick for the best end of the bargain, the gain is hers whoever wins.

But behold how she has endowed man to improve upon all her slack and roundabout methods! She enables him to cheat, and mislead, and circumvent her. He steals her secrets, he tames her very lightnings, he forces her hand on a hundred occasions; he turns her rivers, he levels her hills, he obliterates her marshes, he makes her deserts bloom as the rose; he measures her atoms and surveys and weighs her orbs; he reads her history in the rocks, he finds out her ways in the heavens. He discovers the most completely hidden thing in the universe, the ether, and he has learned how to use it for his own purposes; his wireless telegraphy turns it into a news highway; above the seas, over the mountains, and across continents, it carries his messages.

In man Nature has evolved the human from the unhuman; she has evolved justice and mercy from rapine and cruelty; she has evolved the civic from the domestic, the state from the tribe. She has evolved the Briton and the Frenchman from rude prehistoric man. She has not yet got rid of the Hun in the German, but she is fast getting rid of the German in her overseas Germanic stock. The bleaching process goes on apace.

Man sees where Nature is blind; he takes a straight cut where she goes far around. In him she has added reason to her impulse, conscience to her blind forces, self-denial to her self-indulgence, the power of choice to her iron necessity. How well she has done by man, man alone knows. How much he is dependent upon her, he alone knows; how completely he is a part of her, he alone knows. We may call man an insurgent in her world, as an English scientist does, but he is her insurgent; she inspires him to insurrection, and she puts his weapons in his hands. His cause is her cause, and his victories are her victories.

Only by personifying Nature in this way, and standing apart from her and regarding her objectively, can we contrast her methods and her spirit with our own. The mother she has been to us becomes apparent. In spite of all her short-comings and delays and roundabout methods, here we are, and here we wish to remain.

V

THE GOOD DEVILS

I

THIS is not an essay on the optimism of a moralist, but on the optimism of a naturalist.

On the whole and in the long run, as I am never tired of asserting, Nature is good. The universe has not miscarried. The celestial laws, as Whitman says, do not need to be worked over and rectified. It is good to be here, and it must be equally good to go hence. With all the terrible things in Nature, and all the cruel and wicked things in history, the world is good; life is good, and the Devil himself plays a good part.

When Emerson in his Journal says, "It is very odd that Nature should be so unscrupulous. She is no saint," one wonders just what he means. Does he expect gravity, or fire, or flood, or wind, or tide to have scruples? Should the cat have scruples about dining off the mouse or the bird, or the wolf about making a meal of the lamb? or the plants and trees have scruples about running their roots into one another's preserves, or cutting off one another's rain or sunshine? If our cowbird had the human conscience, we should expect her to have scruples about laying her egg in the nest of another bird and thus shirking the labors and cares of parenthood, and we should expect the jays and crows to have scruples about eating up the eggs and young of their feathered neighbors, if they, too, were endowed with conscience. But none of them are troubled in this way, for the simple reason that they are not human beings. They live below the plane of man's moral conscience. Chemistry and the elementary forces have no scruples. Powder or dynamite will blow up its maker as soon as it will any one else. The rain does not scruple to spoil the farmer's hay, or the floods to wash away his house and destroy its inmates.

We are childish when we marvel at the unscrupulousness of Nature. Emerson often appealed to the nature of things. It is in the nature of things that they should be what we name unscrupulous; certainly Nature "is no saint," and it is well for us that she is not. If we identify Nature with what we call God, as many do, then I am saying that it is well for us that the Eternal is "no saint." I suspect that if the drama of life which has been enacted upon the globe, and is still being enacted, had been modeled upon the principle of sainthood, you and I would not now be here. More's the pity, you may say, but there is no pity in Nature.

II

Is Nature then of the Devil? If we choose to name

it so, — if we choose to revert to the conception of an earlier age, — yes, Nature, as we see her from our limited human point of view, is more or less of the Devil — half god and half demon, we may say; divine in some of her manifestations and diabolical in others, divine when she favors us and diabolical when she is against us. But what we do not so readily see is that in the long run the Devil is on our side also, that he is the divine wearing a mask. The Devil is the absence of something; he is a negative quantity that stimulates the positive and sets and keeps the currents going. Our breathing is the result of a perpetual tendency to a vacuum in our lungs; the growth of our bodies is the result of a coöperation and agreement between the integrating and disintegrating forces.

We control the Devil and make him our friend when we control most of the forces of nature — the fire, the wind, the waters, electricity, magnetism, gravity, chemical affinity, and so on. If our hold upon them slips, they destroy us. If we are not watchful in our laboratories, the same chemistry that builds up our bodies will blow our bodies to atoms. The tornado, the earthquake, the volcano, the thunderbolt, have all helped to make the earth what we behold it. The floods have helped, the avalanches have helped, frost and wind and snow, tropic heat and arctic cold, have helped. These devils are the hod-carriers that serve the divine mason — the mixers and builders, the plowers and the planters, the levelers and the engineer. Hence, I say: "Good Devil, be thou my friend; you give me power, you sharpen my wits, you make a man of me."

This is the tangible, physical Devil; the intangible, moral Devil is not so easily dealt with. It is not so easy to turn the spirit of crime, intemperance, cruelty, war, superstition, greed, and so on to our advantage. Yet there also is power going to waste or misdirected. There is a light under the feet of these things also. Trade, out of which has come greed, has opened up and humanized the world; war has often grafted a superior stock upon an inferior.

"It was for Beauty that the world was made." Emerson quotes this verse from Ben Jonson and says that it is better than any single line of Tennyson's "In Memoriam." Only the poet is allowed to make such extravagant statements. We cannot in soberness and truth say that the world was made for any particular end. It is out of a certain harmony of the elements that we arose and our sense of beauty was developed, but the world exists for as many ends as we have power to conceive. Order, harmony, rhythm, compensation, equilibrium, circles, spheres, are fundamental in nature. Music, which is beauty to the ear, hath power over inert matter. In the Mammoth Cave the very rocks will sing if you speak to them in the right key. How steel filings on a metal surface will dance and arrange themselves in symmetrical groups under the influence of musical chords! Harmony is at the heart of nature, but, in the music of creation, disharmony plays a part also. The world is not all beautiful unless seen as a whole; all its discords are harmonized in the curve of the sphere. Emerson's own line, "Beauty is its own excuse for being," is better and truer than the one he quotes from Ben Jonson.

When saying that in the music of creation disharmony plays a part also, I do not mean to imply that this is not also true in human music. The dissonances are just as much a part of great music as are the harmonies. What would the operas of Wagner be without the tremendous dissonances? That is what makes Wagner one of the greatest in music; he sees things whole, just as Whitman does in his art — sees that "all are but parts of one stupendous whole," and that the merely pretty in music, in poetry, in any art, as in nature, is only one little phase of it, only an arc of the great circle.

III

WHAT trouble we get into when we identify God with Nature! and what trouble we get into when we refuse to identify the two! In the first case we reach the unity that the mind craves, but it is a unity made up of those antagonisms which revolt us. In the second case it is a duality that leaves half of the world to the Devil.

We select what we call the divine and stand confused and abashed before the residue. We must either change our notion about the power we call God and make it all-inclusive, embracing evil as well as good, or else we must change our notion about Nature and see no evil in her. God and Nature are one. If they are two, who or what is the second?

How can we fail to see that all the shaded part of the picture is necessary to the picture — that all high lights would not make a picture, but only a daub; and that all that we call good would not make a world in which men could live and develop? Life goes on under conditions more or less antagonistic. The antagonism gives the power; the friction develops electricity. The vices and crimes and follies and excesses of society are the riot and overflow of the virtues. The pride of the rich, the tyranny of power, the lust of gain, the riot of sensuality, are all a little too much of a good thing — a little too much heat or light or rain or frost or snow or food or drink. There can be no perversions till there is something good to pervert, no counterfeits till there is first the genuine article.

The currents of wild life get out of their banks and we have, for example, a plague of locusts or moths or forest worms, but the natural check surely comes. The military spirit of Germany, which springs from a laudable devotion to the state and to the good of all, got out of its banks and brought on the World War, but the flood has subsided and will probably be so dyked that it can never get out again. It will find its outlet in the arts of peace.

IV

THE so-called laws of Nature were not designed and decreed as our human laws are. There is no great lawgiver. Her laws are a sequence of events and activities; this sequence has worked itself out through countless ages. Nothing in the universe was designed in the human sense: it was not first a thought in some one's mind, then to become an act or a contrivance. This concept does not express the mystery of creation. There is a constant becoming; there was no beginning, there can be no ending. There is perpetual change and revolution, perpetual transfer and promotion, but nothing that can be explained in terms of our human experience and achievement. The world and all it holds were created as the flower is created in the spring, as the snowflake is created in the winter, as the cloud is created in the summer sky. Man was created as the chick is created in the egg. Man has had a long day of creation; he has been becoming man since the first dawn of life in the old Palæozoic seas. His horse and his dog have been becoming what we behold them through all the geologic

ages. This view does not leave the Eternal out of
the universe; it puts Him in it so that He cannot be
got out. It makes Him immanent in it at all points;
it makes Nature transcend human reason and human
speech. As long as we think of God as a kind of
superman external to nature, we can deny Him and
cut Him out, but when we identify ourselves and all
things else with Him, there is no escaping Him. We
ourselves are a phase or a fraction of Him. When
we select or screen out what we name the good, the
fair, the divine, and call that God, what are we to do
with the residue? Call it the Devil? The Devil, too,
then is a part of the Eternal Good. I want no emas-
culated universe. I want the fiber and virility and
pungency and power and heat and drive which all
that we call bad gives it.

Our mission is to tame and elevate and direct the
elements and forces without weakening them.
Thence comes our power. A perfect world would
not be one without sin or suffering or struggle or
failure. There can be no perfect world. But there
can be one more and more livable, more and more
in harmony with those laws that promote our well-
being. Approximations, approximations — that is
our success, and never complete fulfillment! When
we say that God is the All, we must have the courage of our convictions and not flinch at the consequences. He is all that we call bad as well as all
that we call good. What we call good is *our* good,

and not absolute good. There is no absolute good
any more than there is absolute heat or cold or
height or depth.

We work our way through the mazes and contradictions of things — contradictions from our point
of view — as best we can, eliminating the bad and
cleaving unto the good, but the total scheme of
things, the reconciliations and compensations and
final results, we can never grasp. We cannot abate
our war upon evil, because we have our well-being
on these terms, but evil is indirectly the father of
good.

V

ALL religious and ethical systems grow out of our
egoism. We plant ourselves in the middle of the
universe and say it is all for us. We make gods in
our own image, we invent a heaven for the good and
a hell for the wicked, and seek to keep down the
brute within us by a system of rewards and punishments. We improve our minds and souls as we improve the fields; we make them more fair and fertile,
but we do not eliminate Nature; with her own
weapons we improve our relations to her — we promote *our* good, but we are still Nature's; the harvest
we reap is still Nature's. Our improvements upon
her are mere removal of obstructions from the rill
that gushes perennially from her prolific earth. We
improve her fruits, her flowers, her animals — that

is, make them more serviceable to us — by means of the hold we have upon her methods. We add nothing; we utilize what she has placed within our reach. All of which means that we are Nature's, and that our knowing it and thinking of it cannot make the slightest difference. Our fate is inevitable. There is no escape. Whose else could we be? We cannot get off the sphere; if we could, we should still be a part of the All. Our elaborate schemes to appropriate or propitiate the Eternal, to stand well with Him, to gain heaven and avoid hell, are devices of cunning Nature to spur us on the road of development. (How easily one falls into the language of extreme anthropomorphism!) The beautiful myth of the Garden of Eden and the fall of man is full of meaning. Surely it was a good devil that put man in the way of knowing good from evil, and led to his expulsion from a state of innocent impotence.

Nature's dealings with man and with the other forms of life are on the same plan as her dealings with the earth as a whole. The drainage system of the globe is by no means perfect; there are marshes and stagnant waters in every country, but how small comparatively the area they cover! The rains and snows give birth to pure springs in all lands, which unite to form the creeks, which, again, unite to form the rivers, which flow into the lakes and seas, giving back to the great bodies of water what the sun and

the winds took from them, and thus keeping the
vital currents of the globe in ceaseless motion. The
same may be said of the weather system of the
globe; it is not perfect everywhere — too much
rain here, too much sun there, too hot in some parts,
too cold in others, but on the whole favoring life and
development.

We think we could improve the weather. So we
might for our special purposes at times — when it
rains and we have hay down, or a crop to put in, or
a picnic in view; but it is better on the whole that
we adapt ourselves to the weather than that the
weather be adapted to the special needs of each of
us. The Lord would be pretty sure to get mixed up
if He tried the latter plan.

A general and not a special Providence is our salvation. Good and evil mixed make life, as cloud and
sun in due proportions make the best climate.

VI

WAR is a scourge like fire, the whirlwind, the
earthquake, when viewed in the light of a particular
time and people, but good may come from it after
the lapse of ages. It strengthens and consolidates
and develops the heroic virtues. Yet what a legacy
of suffering and death go with it! But to invoke
war is like invoking the pestilence, the tornado, the
earthquake. The guilt of the German military staff
in bringing on the World War is of the blackest dye.

It may be a good to man, but it is a terrible evil to men. We cannot afford to play Providence; we must not play with Jove's thunderbolts. War cannot come to any people unless somebody (or some body of men) wills it, and to will an aggressive war is a crime. No matter if the recent war puts a final end to war, the gods will not credit us with the good that flows from our act over and above our purpose and will.

All the good that comes from war comes from struggle, self-denial, heroism; and all courses of action that develop these traits are substitutes for war. The farm, the mining-camp, engineering, exploration, are substitutes. The best war material is recruited from these fields. The man who can guide the plowshare can wield the sword; the man who can face the grizzly and the lion can face the cannon and the torpedo. War develops no new virtues; it helps rejuvenate the old; obedience, team-work, system, organization and so on are achievements of an industrial age. In history most wrongs are finally righted and the balance is fairly kept, but this is not by the will and purpose of the actors, but by the remedial forces of nature and life.

The guilt falls the same upon the greed and lust of power, even if the gods finally reap a harvest that man's iniquities have sown. He maketh the wicked to praise Him, but the wicked are to get no credit. Here is where our moral standards diverge from those of the natural universal. Our moral standards apply to us alone; they are special and limited. The gods know them not. The rain falls alike upon the just and upon the unjust. The poet says, "I judge not as the judge judges, but as the sunlight falling around a helpless thing." This is the voice of the natural universal. When we judge as the judge judges, we condemn strife and war and all such uncharity, we execute or imprison criminals, we found asylums and hospitals and other charitable organizations; when we judge as Nature or the poet judges, we say to the fallen one:

"Not till the sun excludes you do I exclude you,
Not till the waters refuse to glisten for you and the leaves to
    rustle for you, do my words refuse to glisten and rustle
    for you."

The All brings mercy out of cruelty, love out of hatred, life out of death, but man's orbit is so small that he cannot harmonize these contradictions. The curve of the universal laws does not bring him round till generations have passed. To keep on traveling east till you approach your point of departure from the west, you must have the round globe to travel on. An empire would not avail.

VII

GOOD and evil are strangely mixed in this world, and probably in all other worlds. What is evil to one creature is often good to another. It is an evil to the vireo or to the warbler when the cowbird lays its egg in the nest of one of these birds, but it is a good to the cowbird. It relieves her of all maternal cares, and provides her young with a devoted nurse and stepmother, but the young warblers or vireos are likely to perish. All parasites live at the expense of some other form of life, and are to that extent evils to these forms; but Nature is just as much interested in one form as in the other; an ill wind to one blows good to another, and thus the balance is kept.

A world without evil would be an impossible world — as impossible as mechanical motion without friction or as sunlight without shadow. The two worlds, the organic and the inorganic, constantly interact. The former draws all its elements and its power from the latter, which is passive to it, and goes its way in the inexorable round of physical laws, irrespective of it. Viewed as a whole, the evils of life inhere in its elements and conditions. Air, water, fire, soil, give us our strength and our growth; they also destroy us if we fail to keep right relations to them. We cannot walk or lift a hand without gravity; and yet, give gravity a chance, and it crushes us, the floods drown us, fire consumes us! Could we have life on any other terms; could God himself annul these conditions?

Hunger is or may become an evil destroying life, but does it not imply the opposite condition of good

— food, an appetite, power of assimilation in the organism? Disease is an evil to the living body it attacks, but it does not attack a dead body and it often educates the body to resist disease. It is a war which may leave the victor more capable than he was before.

Robert Ingersoll conceived of an improvement in creation — "make health contagious instead of disease." But this is to trifle with words. In a certain sense health is contagious. But physical health, like peace of mind, is a condition, and must come from harmony within, while a contagious disease is conveyed by a living micro-organism, and is truly catching, and to change or reverse all this would be to destroy the conditions of life itself. To postulate a world in which two and two would make five, or in which a straight line is not the shortest distance between two points, is to take the road to the insane asylum. Evil is positive only in the sense that shadow or darkness is positive, or that cold is positive. It is a greater or lesser degree of negation.

In society and in the state we seek to curb or to correct or to eliminate Nature's errors, and in doing so often fall into other errors and cross-purposes. Yet to fight what we call evil, and promote what we call good, is the supreme duty of all men. Physical evil the doctors and natural philosophers warn us against; moral evil, which is a much more intangible thing, our ethical teachers point out to us; mental evil, ignorance, superstition, false judgment, and so on, the schools and colleges help us to avoid; religious evil, economic evil, political evil, all have their safeguards and guides.

Why could not a world have been made in which there was no evil? In asking such a question we misapprehend the nature of the world; we are thinking of something made and a maker external to it; we are trying the universe by the standards of our human experience. The world was not made, man was not created in any sense paralleled by our human experience with tangible bodies. The world and all there is in it is the result of evolution, or an endless process of creation, an everlasting becoming, in which the nature of things beyond which we can take no step plays the principal part. A world on any other terms would not be the world to which we are adjusted, and out of whose conflicting forces our lives came.

There will be times when the light will blind the eye; other times when the darkness will heal and restore it; when the heat will burn the hand, when the food will poison the stomach, when the friend will weary you, when home is a prison, when books are a bore. Our relations to things make them good or bad: our momentary and accidental relations may make the good things bad, but our permanent natural relations make the good good, the bad bad.

In a world without the gravity which so often

crushes us, we could not walk or lift the hand; without the friction which so often impedes us, our train and vehicles would not move; without the water that could so easily drown us, the currents of our bodies would dry up; without the germs that so often make war upon us, we should soon cease to be. Both friendly and hostile are the powers that surround us, — or, rather, is the power that surrounds us, for it is one and not two, — friendly when we are in the relation to it demanded and provided for by our constitution, and unfriendly when we are in false relation to it. To know this true relation from the false is a part of the discipline of life.

I know this is not the end of the story; there are more questions to be asked. We want a solution of the last solution, but this can never come. Final questions return forever to themselves; they baffle us, constituted as our minds are; they are circles and not lines.

VI

THE NATURAL PROVIDENCE

I

WHAT unthinking people call design in nature is simply the reflection of our inevitable anthropomorphism. Whatever they can use, they think was designed for that purpose — the air to breathe, the water to drink, the soil to plant. It is as if they thought the notch in the mountains was made for the road to pass over, or the bays and harbor for the use of cities and shipping. But in inorganic nature the foot is made to fit the shoe and not the reverse. We are cast in the mould of the environment. If the black cap of the nuthatch which comes to the maple-tree in front of my window and feeds on the suet I place there were a human thinking-cap, the bird would see design in the regular renewal of that bit of suet; he would say, "Some one or something puts that there for me"; but he helps himself and asks no questions. The mystery does not trouble him. Why should not I, poor mortal, feel the same about these blessings and conveniences around me of which I hourly partake, and which seem so providential? Why do not I, with my thinking-cap, infer that some one or something is thinking about me and my well-being? The mass of man-

kind does draw this inference, and it is well for
them to do so. But the case of the bird is different.
The bit of suet that I feed on is not so conspicuously
something extra, something added to the tree; it
is a part of the tree; it is inseparable from it. I am
compelled, as it were, to distil it out of the tree, so
that instead of being the act of a special providence,
it is the inevitable benefaction of the general providence of nature. What the old maple holds for me is
maple-sugar, but it was not put there for me; it is
there just the same, whether I want it or not; it is a
part of the economy of the tree; it is a factor in its
own growth; the tree is not thinking of me (pardon
the term), but of itself. Of course this does not make
my debt to it, and my grounds for thankfulness, any
the less real, but it takes it out of the category of
events such as that which brings the suet to the nuthatch. The Natural Providence is not intermittent,
it is perennial; but it takes no thought of me or you.
It is life that is flexible and adaptive, and not matter
and force. "We do not," says Renan, "remark in
the universe any sign of deliberate and thoughtful
action. We may affirm that no action of this sort has
existed for millions of centuries." I think we may
affirm more than that — we may affirm that it
never existed. Some vestige of the old theology still
clung to Renan's mind — there was a day of creation in which God set the universe going, and then
left it to run itself; the same vestige clung to Dar-

win's mind and led him to say that in the beginning God must have created a few species of animals and vegetables and then left them to develop and populate the world.

Says Renan, "When a chemist arranges an experiment that is to last for years, everything which takes place in his retort is regulated by the laws of absolute unconsciousness; which does not mean that a will has not intervened at the beginning of the experiment, and that it will not intervene at the end." There was no beginning nor will there be any ending to the experiment of creation; the will is as truly there in the behavior of the molecules at one time as at another. The effect of Renan's priestly training and associations clings to him like a birthmark.

In discussing these questions our plumb-line does not touch bottom, because there is no bottom. "In the infinite," says Renan with deeper insight, "negations vanish, contradictions are merged"; in other words, opposites are true. Where I stand on the surface of the sphere is the center of that surface, but that does not prevent the point where you stand being the center also. Every point is a center, and the sky is overhead at one place as at another; opposites are true.

The moral and intellectual worlds present the same contradictions or limitations — the same relatively of what we call truth.

Nature's ways — which with me is the same as saying God's ways — are so different from ours; "no deliberate and thoughtful action," as Renan puts it, no economy of time or material, no short cuts, no cutting-out of non-essentials, no definite plan, no specific ends, few straight lines or right angles; her streams loiter and curve, her forces are unbridled; no loss or gain; her accounts always balance; the loss at one point, or with one form, is a gain with some other — all of which is the same as saying that there is nothing artificial in Nature. All is Natural, all is subject to the hit-and-miss method. The way Nature trims her trees, plants her forests, sows her gardens, is typical of the whole process of the cosmos. God is no better than man because man is a part of God. From our human point of view he is guilty of our excesses and shortcomings. Time does not count, pain does not count, waste does not count. The wonder is that the forests all get planted by this method, the pines in their places, the spruces in theirs, the oaks and maples in theirs; and the trees get trimmed in due time, now and then, it is true, by a very wasteful method. A tree doctor could save and prolong the lives of many of them. The small fountains and streams all find their way to larger streams, and these to still larger, and these to lakes or to the sea, and the drainage system of the continents works itself out with engineering exactitude. The decay of the rocks and the formation of the soil come about in due time, but not in man's time. In all the grand processes and transformations of nature the element of time enters on such a scale as to dwarf all human efforts.

II

WHEN we say of a thing or an event that it was a chance happening, we do not mean that it was not determined by the laws of matter and force, but we mean it was not the result of the human will, or of anything like it; it was not planned or designed by conscious intelligence. Chance in this sense plays a very large part in nature and in life. Though the result of irrefragable laws, the whole non-living world about us shows no purpose or forethought in our human sense. For instance, we are compelled to regard the main features of the earth as matters of chance, the distribution of land and water, of islands and continents, of rivers, lakes, seas, mountains and plains, valleys and hills, the shapes of the continents; that there is more land in the northern hemisphere than in the southern, more land at the South Pole than at the North, is a matter of chance. The serpentine course of a stream through an alluvial plain, a stream two yards wide, winding and ox-bowing precisely as does the Mississippi, is a matter of chance. The whole geography of a country, in fact, is purely a matter of chance, and not the result of anything like human forethought. The planets themselves — that Jupiter is large and

Mercury small; that Saturn has rings; that Jupiter has seven moons; that the Earth has one; that other planets have none; that some of the planets are in a condition to sustain life as we know it, for example, Venus, Earth, and probably Mars; that some revolve in more elliptical orbits than others; that Mercury and Venus apparently always keep the same side toward the sun — all these things are matters of chance. It is easy to say, as did our fathers, that God designed it thus and so, but how are we to think of an omnipotent and omniscient Being as planning such wholesale destruction of his own works as occurs in the cosmic catastrophes which the astronomers now and then witness in the sidereal universe, or even as occur on the earth, when earthquakes and volcanoes devastate fair lands or engulf the islands of the sea? Why should such a Being design a desert, or invent a tornado, or ordain that some portion of the earth's surface should have almost perpetual rain and another portion almost perpetual drought? In Hawaii I saw islands that were green and fertile on one end from daily showers, while the other end, ten miles away, was a rough barren rock, from the entire absence of showers. Were the trade winds designed to bring the vapors of the sea to the tropic lands?

In following this line of thought we, of course, soon get where no step can be taken. Is the universe itself a chance happening? Such a proposition is unthinkable, because something out of nothing is unthinkable. Our experience in this world develops our conceptions of time and space, and to set bounds to either is an impossible task. We say the cosmos must always have existed, and there we stop. We have no faculties to deal with the great ultimate problems.

We are no better off when we turn to the world of living things. Here we see design, particular means adapted to specific ends. Shall we say that a bird or a bee or a flower is a chance happening, as is the rainbow or the sunset cloud or a pearl or a precious stone? Is man himself a chance happening? Here we are stuck and cannot lift our feet. The mystery and the miracle of vitality, as Tyndall called it, is before us. Here is the long, hard road of evolution, the push and the unfolding of life through countless ages, something more than the mechanical and the accidental, though these have played a part; something less than specific plan and purpose, though we seem to catch dim outlines of these.

Spontaneous variations, original adaptations, a never-failing primal push toward higher and more complex forms — how can we, how shall we, read the riddle of it all? How shall we account for man on purely naturalistic grounds?

The consistent exponent of variation cannot go into partnership with supernaturalism. Grant that the organic split off from the inorganic by insensible degrees, yet we are bound to ask what made it split off at all? — and how it was that the first unicellular life contained the promise and the potency of all the life of to-day? Such questions take us into deep waters where our plummet-line finds no bottom. It suits my reason better to say there is no solution than to accept a solution which itself needs solution, and still leaves us where we began.

The adjustment of non-living bodies to each other seems a simple matter, but in considering the adaptations of living bodies to one another, and to their environment, we are confronted with a much harder problem. Life is an active principle, not in the sense that gravity and chemical reactions are active principles, but in a quite different sense. Gravity and chemical reactions are always the same, inflexible and uncompromising; but life is ever variable and adaptive; it will take half a loaf if it cannot get a whole one. Gravity answers yea and nay. Life says, "Probably; we will see about it; we will try again to-morrow." The oak-leaf will become an oak-ball to accommodate an insect that wants a cradle and a nursery for its young; it will develop one kind of a nursery for one insect and another kind for a different insect.

III

As far as I have got, or ever hope to get, toward solving the problem of the universe is to see clearly

that it is insoluble. One can arrive only at negative
conclusions; he comes to see that the problem cannot be dealt with in terms of our human experience and knowledge. But what other terms have
we? Our knowledge does not qualify us in any degree to deal with the Infinite. The sphere has no
handle to take hold of, and the Infinite baffles the
mind in the same way. Measured by our human
standards, it is a series of contradictions. The
method of Nature is a haphazard method, yet behold the final order and completeness! How many
of her seeds she trusts to the winds and the waters,
and her fertilizing pollens and germs also! And the
winds and the waters do her errands, with many
failures, of course, but they hit the mark often
enough to serve her purpose. She provides lavishly
enough to afford her failures.

When we venture upon the winds and the waters
with our crafts, we aim to control them, and we
reach our havens only when we do control them.

What is there in the method of Nature that answers to the human will in such matters? Nothing
that I can see; yet her boats and her balloons reach
their havens — not all of them, but enough of them
for her purpose. Yet when we apply the word "purpose" or "design" to Nature, to the Infinite, we
are describing her in terms of the finite, and thus fall
into contradictions. Still, the wings and balloons
and hooks and springs in the vegetable world are for

a specific purpose — to scatter the seed far from the parent plant. Every part and organ and movement of a living body serves a purpose to that organism. The mountain lily looks straight up to the sky; the meadow lily looks down to the earth; undoubtedly each flower finds its advantage in its own attitude, but what that advantage is, I know not. If Nature planned and invented as man does, she would attain to mere unity and simplicity. It is her blind, prodigal, haphazard methods that result in her endless diversity. When she got a good wing for the seed of a tree, such as that of the maple, she would, if merely efficient, give this to the seeds of other similar trees; but she gives a different wing to the ash, to the linden, to the elm, the pine, and the hemlock, while to some she gives no wings at all. The nut-bearing trees, such as the oaks, the beeches, the walnuts, and the hickories, have no wings, except such as are afforded them by the birds and beasts that feed upon them and carry them away. And here again Nature has a purpose in the edible nut which tempts some creatures to carry it away. If all the nuts were devoured, the whole tribe of nut-bearing trees would in time be exterminated, and Nature's end defeated. But in a world of conflicting forces like ours, chance plays an important part; many of the nuts get scattered, and not all devoured. The hoarding-up propensities of certain birds and squirrels result in the planting of many oaks and chestnuts and beeches.

The inherent tendency to variation in organic life, together with Nature's hit-and-miss method, account for her endless variety on the same plane, as it were, as that of her many devices for disseminating her seeds. One plan of hook or barb serves as well as another, — that of bidens as well as that of hound's-tongue, — yet each has a pattern of its own. The same may be said of the leaves of the trees : their function is to expose the juices of the tree to the chemical action of light and air; yet behold what an endless variety in their shape, size, and structure! This is the way of the Infinite — to multiply endlessly, to give a free rein to the physical forces and let them struggle with one another for the stable equilibrium to which they never, as a whole, attain; to give the same free rein to the organic forces and let their various forms struggle with one another for the unstable equilibrium which is the secret of their life.

The many contingencies that wait upon the circuit of the physical forces and determine the various forms of organic matter — rocks, sand, soil, gravel, mountain, plain — all shifting and changing endlessly — wait upon the circuit of the organic forces and turn the life impulse into myriad channels, and people the earth with myriads of living forms, each accidental from our limited point of view, while all are determined by irrefragable laws. The contradictions in such statements are obvious and are inevitable when the finite tries to measure or describe the ways of the Infinite.

The waters of the globe are forever seeking the repose of a dead level, but when they attain it, if they ever do, the world will be dead. Behold what a career they have in their circuit from the sea to the clouds and back to the earth in the ministering rains, and then to the sea again through the streams and rivers! The mantling snow with its exquisite crystals, the grinding and transporting glaciers, the placid or plowing and turbulent rivers, the sparkling and refreshing streams, the cooling and renewing dews, the softening and protecting vapors, wait upon this circuit of the waters through the agency of the sun, from the sea, through the sky and land, back to the sea again. Yes, and all the myriad forms of life also. This circuit of the waters drives and sustains all the vital machinery of the globe.

Why and how the sun and the rain bring the rose and the violet, the peach and the plum, the wheat and the rye, and the boys and the girls, out of the same elements and conditions that they bring the thistles and the tares, the thorn and the scrub, the fang and the sting, the monkey and the reptile, is the insoluble mystery.

If Nature aspires toward what we call the good in man, does she not equally aspire toward what we call the bad in thorns and weeds and reptiles? May we not say that good is our good, and bad is our bad, and that there is, and can be, no absolute good and no absolute bad, any more than there can be an absolute up or an absolute down?

How haphazard, how fortuitous and uncalculated is all this business of the multiplication of the human race! What freaks, what failures, what monstrosities, what empty vessels, what deformed limbs, what defective brains, what perverted instincts! It is as if in the counsels of the Eternal it had been decided to set going an evolutionary impulse that should inevitably result in man, and then leave him to fail or flourish just as the ten thousand contingencies of the maelstrom of conflicting earth forces should decide, so that whether a man become a cripple or an athlete, a fool or a philosopher, a satyr or a god, is largely a matter of chance. Yet the human brain has steadily grown in size, human mastery over nature has steadily increased, and chance has, upon the whole, brought more good to man than evil. Optimism is a final trait of the Eternal.

And the taking-off of man, how haphazard, how fortuitous it all is! His years shall be threescore and ten; but how few, comparatively, reach that age, how few live out half their days! Disease, accident, stupidity, superstition, cut him off at all ages — in infancy, in childhood, in youth, in manhood; his whole life is a part of the flux and uncertainty of things. No god watches over him aside from himself and his kind, no atom or molecule is partial to him, gravity crushes him, fire burns him, the floods drown him as readily as they do vipers and vermin. He takes his chances, he gains, and he loses, but Nature treats him with the same impartiality that she treats the rest of her creatures. He runs the same gantlet of the hostile physical forces, he pays the same price for his development; but his greater capacity for development — to whom or what does he owe that? If we follow Darwin we shall say natural selection, and natural selection is just as good a god as any other. No matter what we call it, if it brought man to the head of creation and put all things (nearly all) under his feet, it is god enough for anybody. At the heart of it there is still a mystery we cannot grasp. The ways of Nature about us are no less divine because they are near and familiar. The illusion of the rare and the remote, science dispels. Of course we are still trying to describe the Infinite in terms of the finite.

IV

WE are so attached to our kind, and so dependent upon them, that most persons feel homeless and orphaned in a universe where no suggestion of sympathy and interest akin to our own comes to us from the great void. A providence of impersona.

forces, the broadcast, indiscriminate benefits of nature, kind deeds where no thought of kindness is, well-being as the result of immutable law — all such ideas chill and disquiet us, until we have inured ourselves to them. We love to fancy that we see friendly hands and hear friendly voices in nature. It is easy to make ourselves believe that the rains, the warmth, the fruitful seasons, are sent by some Being for our especial benefit. The thought that we are adapted to nature and not nature made or modified to suit us, is distasteful to us. It rubs us the wrong way. We have long been taught to believe that there is air because we have lungs, and water because we need it to drink, and light because we need it to see. Science takes this conceit out of us. The light begat the eye, and the air begat the lungs.

In the universe, as science reveals it to us, sensitive souls experience the cosmic chill; in the universe as our inevitable anthropomorphism shapes it for us, we experience the human glow. The same anthropomorphism has in the past peopled the woods and fields and streams and winds with good and evil spirits, and filled the world with cruel and debasing superstitions; but in our day we have got rid of all of this; we have abolished all gods but one. This one we still fear, and bow down before, and seek to propitiate — not with offerings and sacrifices, but with good Sunday clothes and creeds and pew-rents and praise and incense and surplices and ceremonies. What Brocken shadows our intense personalism casts upon nature! We see the gigantic outlines of our own forms, and mistake them for a veritable god. But as we ourselves are a part of nature, so this humanizing tendency of ours is also a part of nature, a part of human nature — not valid and independent, like the chemical and physical forces, but as valid and real as our dreams, our ideas, our aspirations. All the gods and divinities and spirits with which man has peopled the heavens and the earth are a part of Nature as she manifests herself in our subjective selves. So there we are, on a trail that ends where it began. We condemn one phase of nature through another phase of nature that is active in our own minds. How shall we escape this self-contradiction? As we check or control the gravity without us by the power of the gravity in our own bodies, so our intelligence must sit in judgment on phases of the same Universal Intelligence manifested in outward nature.

It is this recognition of an intelligence in nature akin to our own that gives rise to our anthropomorphism. We recognize in the living world about us the use of specific means to specific ends, and this we call intelligence. It differs from our own in that it is not selective and intensive in the same way. It does not take short cuts; it does not aim at human efficiency; it does not cut out waste and delay and pain. It is the method of trial and error. It hits its mark because it hits all marks. Species succeed because the tide that bears them on is a universal tide. It is not a river, but an ocean current. Nature progresses, but not as man does by discarding one form and adapting a higher. She discards nothing; she keeps all her old forms and ways and out of them evolves the higher; she keeps the fish's fin, while she perfects the bird's wing; she preserves the invertebrate, while she fashions the vertebrate; she achieves man, while she preserves the monkey. She gropes her way like a blind man, but she arrives because all goals are hers. Perceptive intelligence she has given in varying degrees to all creatures, but reasoning intelligence she has given to man alone. I say "given," after our human manner of speaking, when I mean "achieve." There is no giving in Nature — there is effort and development. There is interchange and interaction, but no free gifts. Things are bought with a price. The price of the mind of man — who can estimate what it has been through the biological and geological ages? — a price which his long line of antecedent forms has paid in struggle and suffering and death. The little that has been added to the size of his brain since the Piltdown man and the Neanderthal man — what effort and pain has not that cost? We pay for what we get, or our forbears paid for it. They paid for the size of our brains, and we pay for our progress in knowledge.

V

THE term "religion" is an equivocal and much-abused word, but I am convinced that no man's life is complete without some kind of an emotional experience that may be called religious. Not necessarily so much a definite creed or belief as an attraction and aspiration toward the Infinite, or a feeling of awe and reverence inspired by the contemplation of this wonderful and mysterious universe, something to lift a man above purely selfish and material ends, and open his soul to influences from the highest heavens of thought.

Religion in some form is as natural to man as are eating and sleeping. The mysteries of life and the wonder and terror of the world in which he finds himself, arouse emotions of awe and fear and worship in him as soon as his powers of reflection are born. In man's early history religion, philosophy, and literature are one. He worships before he investigates; he builds temples before he builds schoolhouses or civic halls. He is, of course, superstitious long before he is scientific; he trembles before the supernatural long before he has mastered the natural. The mind of early man was synthetic as our emotions always are; it lumped things, it did not differentiate and classify. The material progress of the race has kept pace with man's power of analysis — the power to separate one thing from another, to resolve things into their component parts and recombine them to serve his own purposes. He gets water power, steam power, electric power, by separating a part from the whole and placing his machinery where they tend to unite again.

Science tends more and more to reveal to us the unity that underlies the diversity of nature. We must have diversity in our practical lives; we must seize Nature by many handles. But our intellectual lives demand unity, demand simplicity amid all this complexity. Our religious lives demand the same. Amid all the diversity of creeds and sects we are coming more and more to see that religion is one, that verbal differences and ceremonies are unimportant, and that the fundamental agreements are alone significant. Religion as a key or passport to some other world has had its day; as a mere set of statements or dogmas about the Infinite mystery it has had its day. Science makes us more and more at home in this world, and is coming more and more, to the intuitional mind, to have a religious value. Science kills credulity and superstition, but to the well-balanced mind it enhances the feeling of wonder, of veneration, and of kinship which we feel in the presence of the marvelous universe. It quiets our fears and apprehensions, it pours oil upon the troubled waters of our lives, and reconciles us to the world as it is. The old fickle and jealous gods begotten by our fears and morbid consciences fall away, and the new gods of law and order, who deal justly if mercilessly, take their places.

"The mind of the universe which we share," is a phrase of Thoreau's — a large and sane idea which shines like a star amid his many firefly conceits and paradoxes. The physical life of each of us is a part or rill of the universal life about us, as surely as every ounce of our strength is a part of gravity. With equal certainty, and under the same law, our mental lives flow from the fountain of universal mind, the cosmic intelligence which guides the rootlets of the smallest plant as it searches the soil for the elements it needs, and the most minute insect in availing itself of the things it needs. It is this primal current of life, the two different phases of which we see in our bodies and in our minds, that continues after our own special embodiments of it have ceased; in it is the real immortality. The universal mind does not die, the universal life does not go out. The jewel that trembles in the dewdrop, the rain that lends itself to the painting of the prismatic colors of the bow in the clouds, pass away, but their fountain-head in the sea does not pass away. The waters may make the wonderful circuit through the clouds, the air, the earth, and the cells and veins of living things, any number of times — now a globule of vapor in the sky, now a starlike crystal in the snow, now the painted mist of a waterfall, then the limpid current of a mountain brook — and still the sea remains unchanged. And though the life and mentality of the globe passes daily and is daily renewed, the primal source of those things is as abounding as ever. It is not you and I that are immortal; it is Creative Energy, of which we are a part. Our immortality is swallowed up in this.

The poets, the prophets, the martyrs, the heroes, the saints — where are they? Each was but a jewel in the dew, the rain, the snowflake — throbbing, burning, flashing with color for a brief time and then vanishing, adorning the world for a moment and then caught away into the great abyss. "O spendthrift Nature!" our hearts cry out; but Nature's spending is only the ceaseless merging of one form into another without diminution of her material or blurring of her types. Flowers bloom and flowers fade, the seasons come and the seasons go, men are born and men die, the world mourns for its saints and heroes, its poets and saviors, but Nature remains and is as young and spontaneous and inexhaustible as ever. Where is the comfort in all this to you and to me? There is none, save the comfort or satisfaction of knowing things as they are. We shall feel more at ease in Zion when we learn to distinguish substance from shadow, and to grasp the true significance of the world of which we form a part. In the end each of us will have had his day, and can say as Whitman does,

"I have positively appeared. That is enough."

In us or through us the Primal Mind will have contemplated and enjoyed its own works and will continue to do so as long as human life endures on this planet. It will have achieved the miracle of the Incarnation, and have tasted the sweet and the bitter, the victories and the defeats of evolution. The legend of the birth and life of Jesus is but this everpresent naturalism written large with parable and miracle on the pages of our religious history. In the lives of each of us the supreme reality comes down to earth and takes on the human form and suffers all the struggles and pains and humiliations of mortal, finite life. Even the Christian theory of the vicarious atonement is not without its basis of naturalism. Men, through disease and ignorance and half knowledge, store up an experience that saves future generations from suffering and failure. We win victories for our descendants, and bring the kingdom nearer for them by the devils and evil spirits we overcome.

VII

THE FAITH OF A NATURALIST

I

TO say that man is as good as God would to most persons seem like blasphemy; but to say that man is as good as Nature would disturb no one. Man is a part of Nature, or a phase of Nature, and shares in what we call her imperfections. But what is Nature a part of, or a phase of? — and what or who is its author? Is it not true that this earth which is so familiar to us is as good as yonder morning or evening star and made of the same stuff? — just as much in the heavens, just as truly a celestial abode as it is? Venus seems to us like a great jewel in the crown of night or morning. From Venus the earth would seem like a still larger jewel. The heavens seem afar off and free from all stains and impurities of earth; we lift our eyes and our hearts to them as to the face of the Eternal, but our science reveals no body or place there so suitable for human abode and human happiness as this earth. In fact, this planet is the only desirable heaven of which we have any clue. Innumerable other worlds exist in the abysses of space which may be the abodes of beings superior, and of beings inferior, to ourselves. We place our gods afar off so as to dehumanize them, never suspecting that when we do so we discount their divinity. The more human we are,—remembering that to err is human,—the nearer God we are. Of course good and bad are human concepts and are a verdict upon created things as they stand related to us, promoting or hindering our wellbeing. In the councils of the Eternal there is apparently no such distinction.

Man is not only as good as God; some men are a good deal better, that is, from our point of view; they attain a degree of excellence of which there is no hint in nature — moral excellence. It is not until we treat man as a part of nature — as a product of the earth as literally as are the trees — that we can reconcile these contradictions. If we could build up a composite man out of all the peoples of the earth, including even the Prussians, he would represent fairly well the God in nature.

Communing with God is communing with our own hearts, our own best selves, not with something foreign and accidental. Saints and devotees have gone into the wilderness to find God; of course they took God with them, and the silence and detachment enabled them to hear the still, small voice of their own souls, as one hears the ticking of his own watch in the stillness of the night. We are not cut off, we are not isolated points; the great currents flow through us and over us and around us, and unite us to the whole of nature. Moses saw God in the burning bush, saw him with the eyes of early man whose divinities were clothed in the extraordinary, the fearful, or the terrible; we see him in the meanest weed that grows, and hear him in the gentle murmur of our own heart's blood. The language of devotion and religious conviction is only the language of soberness and truth written large and aflame with emotion.

Man goes away from home searching for the gods he carries with him always. Man can know and feel and love only man. There is a deal of sound psychology in the new religion called Christian Science — in that part which emphasizes the power of the mind over the body, and the fact that the world is largely what we make it, that evil is only the shadow of good — old truths reburnished. This helps us to understand the hold it has taken upon such a large number of admirable persons. Good and evil are relative terms, but evil is only the shadow of good. Disease is a reality, but not in the same sense that health is a reality. Positive and negative electricity are both facts, but positive and negative good belong to a different order. Christian Science will not keep the distemper out of the house if the sewer-gas gets in; inoculation will do more to prevent typhoid and diphtheria than "declaring the truth" or saying your prayers or counting your beads. In its therapeutical value experimental science is the only safe guide in dealing with human corporal ailments.

THE FAITH OF A NATURALIST

We need not fear alienation from God. I feed Him when I feed a beggar. I serve Him when I serve my neighbor. I love Him when I love my friend. I praise Him when I praise the wise and good of any race or time. I shun Him when I shun the leper. I forgive Him when I forgive my enemies. I wound Him when I wound a human being. I forget Him when I forget my duty to others. If I am cruel or unjust or resentful or envious or inhospitable toward any man, woman, or child, I am guilty of all these things toward God: "Inasmuch as ye have done it unto one of the least of these my brethren, ye have done it unto me."

II

I AM persuaded that a man without religion falls short of the proper human ideal. Religion, as I use the term, is a spiritual flowering, and the man who has it not is like a plant that never blooms. The mind that does not open and unfold its religious sensibilities in the sunshine of this infinite and spiritual universe, is to be pitied. Men of science do well enough with no other religion than the love of truth, for this is indirectly a love of God. The astronomer, the geologist, the biologist, tracing the footsteps of the Creative Energy throughout the universe — what need has he of any formal, patent-right religion? Were not Darwin, Huxley, Tyndall, and Lyall, and all other seekers and verifiers of natural truth among the most truly religious of men? Any of these men would have gone to hell for the truth — not the truth of creeds and rituals, but the truth as it exists in the councils of the Eternal, and as it is written in the laws of matter and of life.

For my part I had a thousand times rather have Huxley's religion than that of the bishops who sought to discredit him, or Bruno's than that of the church that burnt him. The religion of a man that has no other aim than his own personal safety from some real or imaginary future calamity, is of the selfish, ignoble kind.

Amid the decay of creeds, love of nature has high religious value. This has saved many persons in this world — saved them from mammon-worship, and from the frivolity and insincerity of the crowd. It has made their lives placid and sweet. It has given them an inexhaustible field for inquiry, for enjoyment, for the exercise of all their powers, and in the end has not left them soured and dissatisfied. It has made them contented and at home wherever they are in nature — in the house not made with hands. This house is their church, and the rocks and the hills are the altars, and the creed is written in the leaves of the trees and in the flowers of the field and in the sands of the shore. A new creed every day and new preachers, and holy days all the week through. Every walk to the woods is a religious rite, every bath in the stream is a saving ordinance.

THE FAITH OF A NATURALIST

Communion service is at all hours, and the bread and wine are from the heart and marrow of Mother Earth. There are no heretics in Nature's church; all are believers, all are communicants. The beauty of natural religion is that you have it all the time; you do not have to seek it afar off in myths and legends, in catacombs, in garbled texts, in miracles of dead saints or wine-bibbing friars. It is of to-day; it is now and here; it is everywhere. The crickets chirp it, the birds sing it, the breezes chant it, the thunder proclaims it, the streams murmur it, the unaffected man lives it. Its incense rises from the plowed fields, it is on the morning breeze, it is in the forest breath and in the spray of the wave. The frosts write it in exquisite characters, the dews impearl it, and the rainbow paints it on the cloud. It is not an insurance policy underwritten by a bishop or a priest; it is not even a faith; it is a love, an enthusiasm, a consecration to natural truth.

The God of sunshine and of storms speaks a less equivocal language than the God of revelation.

Our fathers had their religion and their fathers had theirs, but they were not ours, and could not be in those days and under those conditions. But their religions lifted them above themselves; they healed their wounds; they consoled them for many of the failures and disappointments of this world; they developed character; they tempered the steel in their nature. How childish to us seems the plan of salva-

117

ACCEPTING THE UNIVERSE

tion, as our fathers found it in the fervid and, I freely say, inspired utterances of Saint Paul! But it saved them, it built character, it made life serious, it was an heroic creed which has lost credence in our more knowing and more frivolous age. We see how impossible it is, but we do not see the great natural truths upon which it rests.

A man is not saved by the truth of the things he believes, but by the truth of his belief — its sincerity, its harmony with his character. The absurdities of the popular religions do not matter; what matters is the lukewarm belief, the empty forms, the shallow conceptions of life and duty. We are prone to think that if the creed is false, the religion is false. Religion is an emotion, an inspiration, a feeling of the Infinite, and may have its root in any creed or in no creed. What can be more unphilosophical than the doctrines of the Christian Scientists? Yet Christian Science is a good practical religion. It makes people cheerful, happy, and helpful — yes, and helps make them healthy too. Its keynote is love, and love holds the universe together. Any creed that ennobles character and opens a door or a window upon the deeper meanings of this marvelous universe is good enough to live by, and good enough to die by. The Japanese-Chinese religion of ancestor worship, sincerely and devoutly held, is better than the veneer of much of our fashionable well-dressed religion.

THE FAITH OF A NATURALIST

Guided by appearances alone, how surely we should come to look upon the sun as a mere appendage of the earth! — as much so as is the moon. How near it seems at sunrise and sunset, and as if these phenomena directly involved the sun, extending to it and modifying its light and heat! We do not realize that these are merely terrestrial phenomena, and that the sun, so to speak, knows them not.

Viewed from the sun the earth is a mere speck in the sky, and the amount of the total light and heat from the sun that is received on the earth is so small that the mind can hardly grasp it. Yet for all practical purposes the sun shines for us alone. Our relation to it could not be any more direct and sustaining if it were created for that purpose. It is immanent in the life of the globe. It is the source of all our energy and therefore of our life. Its bounties are universal. The other planets find it is their sun also. It is as special and private to them as to us. We think the sun paints the bow on the cloud, but the bow follows from the laws of optics. The sun knows it not.

It is the same with what we call God. His bounty is of the same universal, impersonal kind, and yet for all practical purposes it exists especially for us, it is immanent every moment in our lives. There is no special Providence. Nature sends the rain upon the just and the unjust, upon the sea as upon the land. We are here and find life good because Providence is general and not special. The conditions are not too easy, the struggle has made men of us. The bitter has tempered the sweet. Evil has put us on our guard and keeps us so. We pay for what we get.

III

THAT wise old Roman, Marcus Aurelius, says, "Nothing is evil which is according to nature." At that moment he is thinking especially of death which, when it comes in the course of nature, is not an evil, unless life itself is also an evil. After the lamp of life is burned out, death is not an evil, rather is it a good. But premature death, death by accident or disease, before a man has done his work or used up his capital of vitality, is an evil. Disease itself is an evil, but if we lived according to nature there would be no disease; we should die the natural, painless death of old age. Of course there is no such thing as absolute evil or absolute good. Evil is that which is against our well-being, and good is that which promotes it. We always postulate the existence of life when we speak of good and evil. Excesses in nature are evil to us because they bring destruction and death in their train. They are disharmonies in the scheme of things, because they frustrate and bring to naught. The war which Marcus Aurelius was waging when he wrote those passages was an evil in itself, though good might come out of it.

THE FAITH OF A NATURALIST

Everything in organic nature — trees, grasses, flowers, insects, fishes, mammals — is beset by evil of some kind. The natural order is good because it brought us here and keeps us here, but evil has always dogged our footsteps. Leaf-blight is an evil to the tree, smallpox is an evil to man, frost is an evil to the insects, flood an evil to the fishes.

Moral evil — hatred, envy, greed, lying, cruelty, cheating — is of another order. These vices have no existence below the human sphere. We call them evils because they are disharmonies; they are inimical to the highest standard of human happiness and well-being. They make a man less a man, they work discord and develop needless friction. Sand in the engine of your car and water in the gasoline are evils, and malice and jealousy and selfishness in your heart are analogous evils.

In our day we read the problem of Nature and God in a new light, the light of science, or of emancipated human reason, and the old myths mean little to us. We accept Nature as we find it, and do not crave the intervention of a God that sits behind and is superior to it. The self-activity of the cosmos suffices. We accept the tornadoes and earthquakes and world wars, and do not lose faith. We arm ourselves against them as best we can. We accept the bounty of the rain, the sunshine, the soil, the changing seasons, and the vast armory of non-living forces, and from them equip or teach ourselves to escape, endure, modify, or ward off the destructive and non-human forces that beset our way. We draw our strength from the Nature that seems and is so regardless of us; our health and wholeness are its gifts. The biologic ages, with all their carnival of huge and monstrous forms, had our well-being at heart. The evils and dangers that beset our way have been outmatched by the good and the helpful. The deep-sea fish would burst and die if brought to the surface; the surface life would be crushed and killed in the deep sea. Life adapts itself to its environment; hard conditions make it hard. Winds, floods, inclement seasons, have driven it around the earth; the severer the cold, the thicker the fur; compensations always abound. If Nature is not all-wise and all-merciful from our human point of view, she has placed us in a world where our own wisdom and mercy can be developed; she has sent us to a school in which we learn to see her own shortcomings and imperfections, and to profit by them.

The unreasoning, unforeseeing animals suffer more from the accidents of nature — drought, flood, lightning — than man does; but man suffers more from evils of his own making — war, greed, intemperance, pestilence — so that the development in both lines goes on, and life is still at the flood.

Good and evil are inseparable. We cannot have

light without shade, or warmth without cold, or life without death, or development without struggle. The struggle for life, of which Darwinism makes so much, is only the struggle of the chick to get out of the shell, or of the flower to burst its bud, or of the root to penetrate the soil. It is not the struggle of battle and hate — the justification of war and usurpation — it is for the most part a beneficent struggle with the environment, in which the fittest of the individual units of a species survive, but in which the strong and the feeble, the great and the small of species alike survive. The lamb survives with the lion, the wren with the eagle, the Esquimo with the European — all manner of small and delicate forms survive with the great and robust. One species of carnivora, or of rodents, or herbivora, does not, as a rule, exterminate another species. It is true that species prey upon species, that cats eat mice, that hawks eat smaller birds, and that man slays and eats the domestic animals. Probably man alone has exterminated species. But outside of man's doings all the rest belongs to Nature's system of checks and balances, and bears no analogy to human or inhuman wars and conquests.

Life struggles with matter, the tree struggles with the wind and with other trees. Man struggles with gravity, cold, wet, heat, and all the forces that hinder him. The tiniest plant that grows has to force its root down into the soil; earlier than that it has to burst its shell or case. The corn struggles to lift itself up after the storm has beaten it down; effort, effort, everywhere in the organic world. Says Whitman:

> "Urge and urge and urge,
> Always the procreant urge of the world."

IV

Every few years we have an ice-storm or a snowstorm that breaks down and disfigures the trees. Some trees suffer much more than others. The storm goes its way; the laws of physical force prevail; the great world of mechanical forces is let loose upon the small world of vital forces; occasionally a tree is so crushed that it never entirely recovers; but after many years the woods and groves have repaired the damages and taken on their wonted thrifty appearance. The evil was only temporary; the world of trees has suffered no permanent setback. But had the trees been conscious beings, what a deal of suffering they would have experienced! An analogous visitation to human communities entails a heritage of misery, but in time it too is forgotten and its scars healed. Fire, blood, war, epidemics, earthquakes, are such visitations, but the race survives them and reaps good from them.

We say that Nature cares nothing for the individual, but only for the race or the species. The whole organic world is at war with the inorganic, and as in human wars the individuals are sacrificed that the army, the whole, may live; so in the strife and competition of nature, the separate units fall that the mass may prosper.

It is probably true that in the course of the biological history of the earth, whole species have been rendered extinct by parasites, or by changing outward conditions. But this has been the exception, and not the rule. The chestnut blight now seems to threaten the very existence of this species of tree in this country, but I think the chances are that this fungus will meet with some natural check.

In early summer comes the June drop of apples. The trees start with more fruit than they can carry, and if they are in vigorous health, they will drop the surplus. It is a striking illustration of Nature's methods. The tree does its own thinning. But if not at the top of its condition, it fails to do this. It takes health and strength simply to let go; only a living tree drops its fruit or its leaves; only a growing man drops his outgrown opinions.

If we put ourselves in the place of the dropped apples, we must look upon our fate as unmixed evil. If we put ourselves in the place of the tree and of the apples that remain on it, the June drop would appear an unmixed good — finer fruit, and a healthier, longer-lived tree results. Nature does not work so much to specific as to universal ends. The individual may go, but the type must remain. The ranks may be decimated, but the army and its cause must triumph. Life in all its forms is a warfare only in the sense that it is a struggle with its outward conditions, in which, other things being equal, the strongest force prevails. Small and weak forms prevail also, because the competing forms are small and weak, or because at the feast of life there is a place for the small and weak also. But lion against lion, man against man, mouse against mouse, the strongest will, in the end, be the victor.

Man's effort is to save waste, to reduce friction, to take short cuts, to make smooth the way, to seize the advantage, to economize time, but the physical forces know none of these things.

Go into the woods and behold the evil the trees have to contend with — all typical of the evil we have to contend with — too crowded in places, one tree crushing another by its fall, specimens on every hand whose term of life might be lengthened by a little wise surgery; borers, blight, disease, insect pests, storm, wreckage, thunderbolt scars, or destruction — evil in a hundred forms besetting every tree, and sooner or later leaving its mark. A few escape — oaks, maples, pines, elms — and reach a greater age than the others, but they fail at last, and when they have rounded out their green century, or ten centuries, and go down in a gale, or in the stillness of a summer night, how often younger trees are marred or crushed by their fall! But come back after many long years, and their places are filled, and all the scars are healed. The new generation of trees is feeding upon the accumulations of the old. Evil is turned to good. The destruction of the cyclone, the ravages of fire, the wreckage of the ice-storm, are all obliterated and the forest-spirit is rank and full again.

There is no wholesale exemption from this rule of waste and struggle in this world, nor probably in any other. We have life on these terms. The organic world develops under pressure from within and from without. Rain brings the perils of rain, fire brings the perils of fire, power brings the perils of power. The great laws go our way, but they will break us or rend us if we fail to keep step with them. Unmixed good is a dream; unmixed happiness is a dream; perfection is a dream; heaven and hell are both dreams of our mixed and struggling lives, the one the outcome of our aspirations for the good, the other the outcome of our fear of evil.

The trees in the woods, the plants in the fields encounter hostile forces the year through; storms crash or overthrow them; visible and invisible enemies prey upon them; yet are the fields clothed in verdure and the hills and plains mantled with superb forests. Nature's haphazard planting and sowing and her wasteful weeding and trimming do not result in failure as these methods do with us. A failure of hers with one form or species results in the success of some other form. All successes are hers.

Allow time enough and the forest returns in the path of the tornado, but maybe with other species of trees. The birds and squirrels plant oaks and chestnuts amid the pines and the winds plant pines amid the oaks and chestnuts. The robins and the cedarbirds sow the red cedar broadcast over the landscape, and plant the Virginia creeper and the poisonivy by every stub and fence-post. The poison-ivy is a triumph of Nature as truly as is the grapevine or the morning-glory. All are hers. Man specializes; he selects this or that, selects the wheat and rejects the tares; but Nature generalizes; she has the artist's disinterestedness; all is good; all are parts of her scheme. She nourishes the foul-smelling catbrier as carefully as she does the rose. Each creature, with man at the head, says, "The world is mine; it was created for me." Evidently it was created for all, at least all forms are at home here. Nature's system of checks and balances preserves her working equilibrium. If a species of forest worm under some exceptionally favoring conditions gets such a start that it threatens to destroy our beech and maple forests, presently a parasite, stimulated by this turn in its favor, appears and restores the balance. For two or three seasons the beech-woods in my native town were ravaged by some kind of worm or beetle; in midsummer the sunlight came into them as if the roof had been taken off; later they swarmed with white millers. But the scourge was suddenly checked

— some parasite, probably a species of ichneumon-fly, was on hand to curtail the dangerous excess.

I am only trying to say that after we have painted Nature as black as the case will allow, after we have depicted her as a savage beast, a devastating storm, a scorching desert, a consuming fire, an all-engulfing earthquake, or as war, pestilence, famine, we have only depicted her from our limited human point of view. But even from that point of view the favoring conditions of life are so many, living bodies are so adaptive, the lift of the evolutionary impulse is so unconquerable, the elemental laws and forces are so overwhelmingly on our side, that our position in the universe is still an enviable one. "Though he slay me, yet will I trust in him." Slain, I shall nourish some other form of life, and the books will still balance — not my books, but the vast ledgers of the Eternal.

In the old times we accounted for creation in the simple terms of the Hebrew Scriptures — "In the beginning God created the heaven and the earth." We even saw no discrepancy in the tradition that creation took place in the spring. But when we attempt to account for creation in the terms of science or naturalism, the problem is far from being so simple. We have not so tangible a point from which to start. It is as if we were trying to find the end or the beginning of the circle. Round and round we go, caught in the endless and begin-

ningless currents of the Creative Energy; no fixity
or finality anywhere; rest and motion, great and
small, up and down, heat and cold, good and evil,
near and far, only relative; cause and effect merging
and losing themselves in each other; life and death
perpetually playing into each other's hands; interior
within interior; depth beneath depth; height above
height; the tangible thrilled and vibrating with the
intangible; the material in bonds to the non-mate-
rial; invisible, impalpable forces streaming around
us and through us; perpetual change and transformation on every hand; every day a day of creation, every night a revelation of unspeakable grandeur; suns and systems forming in the cyclones of
stardust; the whole starry host of heaven flowing
like a meadow brook, but where, or whence, who can
tell? The center everywhere, the circumference nowhere; pain and pleasure, good and evil, inextricably mixed; the fall of man a daily and hourly occurrence; the redemption of man, the same! Heaven or
hell waiting by every doorstep, boundless, beginningless, unspeakable, immeasurable — what wonder that we seek a short cut through this wilderness
and appeal to the supernatural?

When I look forth upon the world and see how,
regardless of man and his well-being, the operations
of Nature go on — how the winds and the storms
wreck him or destroy him, how the drought or the
floods bring to naught his industries, how not the

least force in heaven or earth turns aside for him, or makes any exception to him; in short, how all forms of life are perpetually ground between the upper and the nether millstones of the contending and clashing natural material forces, I ask myself: "Is there nothing, then, under the sun, or beyond the sun, that has a stake in our well-being? Is life purely a game of chance, and is it all luck that we are here in a world so richly endowed to meet all our requirements?" Serene Reason answers: "No, it is not luck as in a lottery. It is the good fortune of the whole. It was inherent in the constitution of the whole, and it continues because of its adaptability; life is here because it fits itself into the scheme of things; it is flexible and compromising." We find the world good to be in because we are adapted to it, and not it to us. The vegetable growth upon the rocks where the sea is forever pounding is a type of life; the waves favor its development. Life takes advantage of turbulence as well as of quietude, of drought as well as of floods, of deserts as well as of marshes, of the sea-bottom as well as of the mountain-tops. Both animal and vegetable life trim their sails to the forces that beat upon them. The image of the sail is a good one. Life avails itself of the half-contrary winds; it captures and imprisons their push in its sails; by yielding a little, it makes headway in the teeth of the gale; it gives and takes; without struggle, without opposition, life would not be life.

The sands of the shore do not struggle with the waves, nor the waves with the sands; the buffeting ends where it began. But trees struggle with the wind, fish struggle with the flood, man struggles with his environment; all draw energy from the forces that oppose them. Life gains as it spends; its waste is an investment. Not so with purely material bodies. They are like the clock, they must be perpetually wound from without. A living body is a clock, ~~perpetually~~ self-wound from within.

The faith and composure of the naturalist or naturist are proof against the worst that Nature can do. He sees the cosmic forces only; he sees nothing directly mindful of man, but man himself; he sees the intelligence and beneficence of the universe flowering in man; he sees life as a mysterious issue of the warring element; he sees human consciousness and our sense of right and wrong, of truth and justice, as arising in the evolutionary sequence, and turning and sitting in judgment upon all things; he sees that there can be no life without pain and death; that there can be no harmony without discord; that opposites go hand in hand; that good and evil are inextricably mingled; that the sun and blue sky are still there behind the clouds, unmindful of them; that all is right with the world if we extend our vision deep enough; that the ways of Nature are the ways of God if we do not make God in our own image, and make our comfort and well-being the prime object of Nature. Our comfort and well-being are provided for in the constitution of the world, but we may say that they are not guaranteed; they are contingent upon many things, but the chances are upon our side. He that would save his life shall lose it — lose it in forgetting that the universe is not a close corporation, or a patented article, and that it exists for other ends than our own. But he who can lose his life in the larger life of the whole shall save it in a deeper, truer sense.

VIII

A FALLACY MADE IN GERMANY

DURING the Great War the question was asked, "Do the inexorable laws of evolution apply to human beings as they apply to the lower animals and to plants?" Most assuredly they do, but with a difference. Man is as certainly one of the results of the evolutionary process as is the horse or the dog, the tree or the plant. We are as certain of his animal origin as we can well be of anything in the biological history of the globe. But the inference which has so often been drawn from this fact — namely, that man's development involves the same factors, and is along parallel lines — is a fallacy. That the supremacy of might, which has ruled, and still rules in nature below man, justifies the rule of might in human communities in our day, is an invention of perverted human ambition.

As Nature rules by the law of might, and as man is a part of Nature, why is he not under the same rule? The answer is that man is an exceptional creature; that while he is a part of the animal kingdom, he is a new kind of animal; and while he is the outcome of evolution, like the rest, new factors which are not operative in the orders below him have played a leading part in his later development.

These factors are his reason, which gives him a sense of the true and the false, and his conscience, which gives him a sense of right and wrong. These faculties subordinate the rule of might to the rule of right. They have resulted in the establishment of standards of conduct for individuals, for communities, and for organized governments that do not exist among the lower animal orders, and only in a very limited sense in the lower human orders.

There is no question of right and wrong among the plants of the field, or the trees of the forest, or the birds of the air, or the beasts of the earth — only the question of power to survive; might in the sense of power of adaptation settles the question.

Since the dawn of history man's moral and intellectual faculties have come more and more to the fore, the moral standards always lagging a little behind the intellectual and the æsthetic standards. Among nearly all the more advanced ancient races the concepts of justice, of mercy, and of fair dealing were dull and sluggish in comparison with their intellectual acumen and their artistic achievements. The Greeks would lie and steal and set on foot piratical expeditions against their neighbors, while yet they produced such men as Aristotle and Plato, and such artists as Phidias and Praxiteles.

In our day the whole civilized world was shocked and alarmed by the moral lapse of a great people ranking among the highest in intelligence and material efficiency, suddenly preaching and practicing the doctrine of might over right which prevails in the orders below man. The German philosophers brazenly justified their nation's course in their aggressive war, with all its attendant horrors, by an appeal to the Darwinian doctrines of the struggle for existence, and the consequent survival of the fittest, doctrines which play such a prominent part in biological evolution. The nation suddenly slumped into a barbarism worse than that of their ancestral Huns. The Hun was again triumphant, gloating over the prospect of the rich plunder and the orgies of wine and lust that awaited him in new fields of conquest. It was a spectacle to make the Genius of Humanity veil her face and weep tears of blood.

All that was noble and precious in international relations; standards of conduct that it had taken long generations to achieve; the peace and goodwill of the world; coöperation in scientific fields, and in endeavors toward human betterment — all went by the board before the Teutonic debauch of greed and lust for blood and conquest.

Seriously to discuss in our day the question of the rule of might over right — that force is the arbiter of justice in human relations, except when it is invoked to chastise the offender — seems a waste of time. On how low a plane must a people live whose leaders appeal to the way of the tiger with his prey, or of the boa constrictor with his victim, in establishing relations with other peoples! This ferocious appeal of kaiserism to predatory nature — to "Nature red in tooth and claw" — in order to set itself right before the conscience of mankind, is as fatuous as it is fallacious. If we could reckon without the sense of right and wrong, which has a survival value as real as any form of physical might or power of adaptation, especially with the later civilized nations (except Germany), a different face would be put upon the question. But we cannot. The flood-tide of world democracy and humanity is setting too strongly in that direction, and we can only hope and pray that misguided Germany may in the new generation be caught up and borne forward to new greatness and world usefulness, on the bosom of the same tide.

IX

THE PRICE OF DEVELOPMENT.

I

THE biological law of the supremacy of the strong over the weak, of the fit over the less fit, which prevails throughout the world of living things, gives us pause when it is applied to human history and to the relations of man with man. Yet it is true that the price of development is the struggle for life. The road of evolution is an uphill road. When struggle ceases, progress ceases, and evolution becomes devolution. Our strength is the strength of the obstacles we overcome. The living machine, contrary to the non-living, gains power from the friction it begets.

When we open the book of the biological history of the globe, we find, to begin with, no force but that which we call brute force, no justice but power, no crime but weakness, no law but the law of battle. The victory is to the strong and the race to the swift. And it is well. It is on this plan, as I have so often said, that the life of the globe has come to what we behold it. Man has come to his present estate, the trees in the forest, the grasses and flowers of the field, the birds in the air, the fishes in the sea, have each and all attained their present stage of

THE PRICE OF DEVELOPMENT

development through the operation of this law of
natural competition, and the survival of the fittest.
Though marked by what we call cruelty and injustice, in the totality of its operations it is a beneficent law. If it were not so, how could the world of
living things have attained its present development? If it were a malevolent law, would not life
have suffered shipwreck long ago? The world of
living things and of non-living still merits the primal
approval — "Behold, it is very good!" Not your
good, nor my good, but a general good, the good of
all. Nature's scheme, if we may say she has a
scheme, embraces the totality of things, and that
the totality of things is good who but a born pessi-
mist, a radically negative nature, can deny? Mixed
good undoubtedly it is, but is there, or can there be,
any other good in the universe? Good forever free-
ing itself from the non-good, or from the fetters of
evil — good to eat, to drink, to behold, to live by,
to die by — good for the body, good for the mind,
good for the soul, good in time, and good in eternity?

From solar systems to atoms and molecules, the
greater bodies, the greater forces, prevail over the
lesser, and yet flowers bloom, and life is sweet, sweet
for the minor forms as well as for the major.

Inert matter knows only the laws of force. In the
world of living matter, up to a certain point, the
same rule prevails. In the fields and woods the more
vigorous plants and trees run out the less vigorous.

In the dryer meadows in my section of the Catskills the orange hawkweed completely crowds out the meadow grasses; it plants itself on every square inch of the surface, and every four or five years the farmer has to intervene with his plow to turn the battle in favor of the grass again. In the gardens, unless the gardener take a hand in the game, the weeds choke down or smother all his vegetables. The weeds are rank with original sin and they easily supplant our pampered and cultivated cereals and legumes.

In the animal world there are few exceptions to the rule of the supremacy of power. There is no question of right or wrong, of mercy or cruelty. It is not cruel or unjust for the bird to catch the insect, or for the cat to catch the bird, or for the lion to devour the lamb, or for the big fishes to eat up the little fishes. It is the rule of nature, and never a question of right or wrong.

Biological laws are as remorseless as physical laws. The course of animal evolution through the geologic ages is everywhere marked by the triumph of new and superior forms over the old and inferior forms. Among the lower races of man, our remote savage ancestors, might ruled. The strong and prolific tribes supplanted those that were less so, and, among the nations, up to our own day, the rule of natural competition, or survival of the fittest, has held full sway. Those nations which are

dominant are so by virtue of their superior qualities, physical, moral, or intellectual. It is not a
question of might except in so far as this question
is linked with the question of moral and intellectual
superiority.

Is there, then, no such thing as equity, justice,
fair play in the world? Shall I seize my neighbor's
farm and despoil him of his goods and chattels because I am stronger than he? Shall one state invade and despoil another, or seize its territory, because it is stronger and considers itself more fit to
survive?

The rule of might, as I have said, prevails
throughout the world of matter and of life below
man, and long prevailed in pre-human and human
history. But the old law of nature has been limited
and qualified by a new law which has come into the
world and which is just as truly a biological law in
its application to man as was the old law of might.
I refer to the law of man's moral nature, the source
of right, justice, mercy. The progress of the race
and of the nations is coming more and more to
depend upon the observance of this law. Without
it there is no organization, no coöperation, no commerce, no government. Without it anarchy would
rule, and our civilization would crumble and society
disintegrate.

The moral sense of mankind is now the dominant
fact in human history; the rule of might has been

superseded by the rule of right. It is this sense in the civilized world that has revolted so over-whelmingly against the Prussian military power in precipitating the World War; and this conscience will probably be so developed and intensified by the useless waste and cruelty of the war that such a calamity will never again befall the world. Those nations will become the most powerful that are the most just, the most humane, that develop in the highest degree a world conscience, and realize the most intensely that the nations all belong to one family, in which the good and evil of one are the good and evil of all. What can the progress of civilization mean but the progress of international comity, sympathy, coöperation, fair-dealing; in fact, the fullest recognition of the validity of the ethical laws to which we hold individuals and communities amenable?

History is full of violence, cruelty, injustice, and the triumph of the strong over the weak, wherein the end seemed to justify the means; yet never since the world began did physical might alone make moral right. The sheriff and the hangman have made the doctrine unpopular among individuals — the ethical sense of mankind will in time make it equally unpopular among nations.

Nature is not moral; primitive biological laws are not moral; they are unmoral. There is no moral law until it is born of human intercourse; then it becomes more and more a biological law, more and more prominent in social and national progress. The law of the jungle begins and ends in the jungle; when we translate it into human affairs, we must take the cruelty of the jungle out of it, and read it in terms of beneficent competition. Man is the jungle humanized; the fangs and claws are drawn, and the stealthy spring gives place to open and fair competition.

II

In the Darwinian struggle for existence there is first the struggle with environment, or with the non-living forces — heat, cold, storm, wind, flood; the organic always at war with the inorganic out of which its power comes. The fateful physical and mechanical forces go their way regardless of the life that surrounds them and which draws its energy from them. Gravity would pull down every tree and shrub and every animal that walks or flies. The wind and the storm would flatten down the flowers and grasses and grains like a steam roller, and often succeeds in doing so. See the timothy and wheat and corn struggle to lift themselves again. Behold how the trees grip the rocks and soil, and brace themselves against the wind! This struggle is, of course, not a conscious one. Apart from the original push of life, it can all be explained in terms of physics and chemistry. The bio-chemist will tell you why the plant leans toward the light, and why it rights itself when pressed down; but why or how matter organizes itself into the various living forms is a question before which natural philosophy is dumb. Neither chemistry nor physics can give us the secret of life. The ingenious devices to secure cross-fertilization among certain plants, devices for scattering the seed among others, — the hooks, the wings, the springs, — to me all seem to imply intelligence, not apart from, but inherent in, the things themselves. Power of adaptation — to take advantage of wind and flood, of solid and fluid — is one of the mysterious attributes of life. And yet we know that vegetable life takes advantage of these things not, as we do, by forethought and invention, but by a mysterious inherent impulse.

How the bee and the bird battle with the wind, the fish with the waves and the rapids, the fur-bearers with the cold and the snow! how all living creatures struggle to escape or resist the dissolving power of the natural forces!

The ever-present instinct of fear in all wild creatures and in children, and the quickness with which it can be aroused in all persons, throw light upon the crueler aspects of this struggle for existence which is common to all forms of animal life. Had life never been beset with perils, we should have been strangers to the emotion of fear, as would all other creatures. Even the fly that alights on my paper as I write fears my hand. It is ever on guard against its natural enemies. This is the proof of the universal struggle. Among the lower forms the struggle or competition of the fleet with the slow, the cunning with the stupid, the sharp-eyed, the sharp-eared, and the keen of scent with those less so; of the miscellaneous feeders with the more specialized feeders; and, among mankind, the competition of men of purpose, of foresight, of judgment, of experience, of probity, and of other personal resources, with men who are deficient in these things; and, among nations and peoples, the inevitable competition of those who cherish the highest national ideals, the best-organized governments, the best race inheritance, the most natural resources, and so on, with the less fortunate in these respects — all this struggle and competition, I say, is beneficent and on the road to progress.

Myriads of different types of animal and vegetable life fit into the scheme of organic nature without conflict or hindrance, but when there is conflict, the strong prevail. The small and the gigantic, the feeble and the mighty, the timid and the bold, the frail and the robust — birds, insects, mice, squirrels, cattle — exist in the same landscape and all prosper. Only when there is rivalry do the feeble go to the wall, which means only that their numbers are kept down. The cats do not exterminate the mice and rats, nor do the hawks and owls exterminate the other birds; they are a natural check on their undue increase. Nature's checks and balances are all important. When species subsist upon species, as weasels upon rodents and hawks upon other birds, there seems to be some law that keeps the bloodthirsty in check. Why should there be so few weasels, since they appear as prolific as their victims? Why so few pigeon hawks, since the hawks have no natural enemies, while the trees swarm with finches and robins?

The conflicting interests in Nature sooner or later adjust themselves; her checks and balances bring about her equilibrium. In vegetation rivalries and antagonisms bring about adaptations. The mosses and the ferns and the tender wood plants grow beneath the oaks and the pines and are favored by the shade and protection which the latter afford them. The farmer's seeding of grass and clover takes better under the shade of the oats than it would upon the naked ground. In Africa some species of flesh-eaters live upon the leavings of larger and stronger species, and in the tropics certain birds become benefactors of the cattle by preying upon the insects that pester them. Fabre tells of certain insect hosts that blindly favor the parasites that destroy them. The scheme has worked itself out that way and Nature is satisfied. Victim or victor, host or parasite, it is all one to her. Life goes on, and all forms of it are hers.

THE PRICE OF DEVELOPMENT

It is easy to see why the wild plants run out the cultivated ones — the latter are the result of artificial selection. No favor has been shown the wild ones, and hence only the most vigorous have survived. The cultivated plants always have a greater burden to bear than the wild ones, and man helps them to bear it, or, rather, he saddles it upon them. The cultivated races of man have burdens to bear also, much greater than the savage tribes, but this is more than made up to them by their superior brain power, which brain power again has come about in the struggle for existence. Wild tribes have also been under the discipline of natural selection, but by reason of some obscure factors of race or climate or geography they have not profited as have the European and Asiatic races. Their moral natures are more rudimentary.

Doubtless some obscure or unknown factors in the original germ-cells, far back in biological times, caused the divergence and splitting-up of animal forms, and gave to one an impulse that carried it higher in the scale of development than its fellows, just as the same thing happens in human families in our own times. Why some creatures are higher and some are lower, why some eventuated in the bird and some in toad and frog and snake and lizard, is one of the mysteries. In seeking the explanation of these things on natural grounds we are compelled to resort to the fertile expedient of conjecture, and pack the germ with many possibilities, each one depending for its development upon chance occurrence or conditions.

Besides this struggle with the environment there is the struggle of individuals and of species with one another — of oak with oak, of beech with beech, of plant with its kind, for the moisture and nutriment in the soil; of robin with robin for insects and fruit, of fox with fox for mice and rabbits, and of lion with lion for antelope and zebra. I say "struggle," but it is rarely struggle in the sense of strife or battle, but in the sense of natural competition — the victory is to the most lucky and the most vigorous — the sharpest eye, the quickest ear, the most nimble foot; and those most favored by fortune win.

Under the law of variation some individuals have a fuller endowment of vital energy than others; under a severe strain and trial of whatever kind the favored ones will survive, while the others perish. Some men, some animals, can endure more hardships than others; under the same conditions all will not starve or freeze or fall exhausted by the wayside at the same time. In the vegetable world the same inequality in the gift of life exists, though not in the same degree. Some seeds will lie dormant in the soil longer than others of the same kind, and some kinds longer than others. Some seeds will not sprout after the second year, but a few may sprout after the third or even the fourth year. The stream of life is not of uniform depth and fullness; it is shallow in some places, and deep in others, as regards both species and individuals. In the natural competition which goes on all around us, the strongest, the fittest, win in the game, not necessarily by violence, but because, apart from the rôle played by chance, they carry more pounds of vital pressure. Not all acorns become oaks, probably not one in thousands; not all bird's eggs become birds; occasionally one egg in the nest does not hatch, probably because of some defect in fertilization. Some nests are torn out of the trees by storms, or are robbed by crows or jays or squirrels; they were not well hidden. A large percentage of nests on the ground is destroyed by night prowlers or by day prowlers; chance again plays a great part here. Only a small fraction of the spawn of fishes hatches, and a still smaller percentage of the hatched ever reaches maturity. Fortune, good or bad, plays a great part with all forms of life. The acorn that becomes an oak owes much to chance — chance of position and soil, and chance of the vicissitudes of the woods and fields. Falling trees or branches, or the foot of a passing animal, may crush or deform it, or a squirrel or a raccoon devour it. Barring these accidents, it owes, or may owe, not a little to its inherent vitality — to its real oakhood.

The natural competition, or the struggle for

existence among mankind, is of similar character, though on the whole less fortuitous. Coöperation, knowledge, altruism, have done much to eliminate the element of chance. An acorn becomes an oak where ten thousand other acorns fail, mainly by luck, while the child becomes the man mainly through the care and nurture of his parents and of the community in which he lives, but he reaches a position of power and prominence largely through his inherent capabilities. Fortune plays a part here also, as it did with Lincoln and Lee and Grant, but these men all had the native endowment upon which Fortune could build.

In the natural competition that goes on in every town and city, the success of one man over another is not, as a rule, the result of violence or wrong; men of high purpose and character in business and professional life add to the positive wealth and well-being of all; they often lift the whole community to a higher and better standard of living; the unfit profit by the achievements of the fit. The men who have added to the wealth and well-being of this country could be counted by the thousands. It is also true that the men who have accumulated their millions at the expense of others, by fraud and chicanery, or have diverted the earnings of others into their own coffers, could be counted by the thousands. It is this class of men who make the poor poorer. But did the achievements of such men as the late James J. Hill make the poor poorer? Such men add enormously to the wealth of the nation.

With all its discounts and set-backs, the natural struggle for existence has carried the whole race forward. Even business competition may be entirely beneficent. Two men open shops or houses in similar lines in the same town and one outstrips the other. Maybe his location is the better; one side of a street may be more favorable to success than the other side. Maybe he is more affable in manner, more thorough in his methods, more accommodating, more fair-minded, of sounder judgment — in fact, the better man in a beneficent sense.

On a broad view, throughout any country, this will be found to be true: success in business, in the professions, on the farm, in the manufactory, comes to those who deserve it. It cannot be otherwise. The world is thus made. Among the nations the same rule holds. England has earned all the power she has got. She is endowed with the gift of empire. Solid merit alone tells in the long run, as well among nations as among individual men. The worth of France rests upon solid qualities. The worth of Germany is inherent in the character of her people. That she has run to Krupp guns and Kaiserism during these later generations, and has coveted the land and the gold of her neighbors, is one of those human calamities analogous to tornadoes and earthquakes.

In the course of modern history, race supplants race, not so much by force of arms as by force of brain. The Europeans know how to utilize the natural forces and make the stars fight on their side. So far as they have done it by wars of conquest, they have violated the great moral law and the law of natural competition. All wars of conquest by civilized nations are wicked wars. They are becoming more and more odious to mankind, and are bound to become still more so, till they cease entirely. A century ago the conduct of Germany in the recent war would have shocked mankind far less than it has to-day. A century hence such an exhibition of the rule of the jungle among civilized peoples will be impossible. If Germany could ever come to be the dominant power in Europe, it would be through the law of natural competition. Her superior efficiency in the arts of peace, could alone give her the victory. It would have given her the victory in her own age had she been contented with its slow but sure operation.

III

THE question of right and wrong must have emerged, so as to become a factor in the evolution of human society, very slowly — how slowly, we can never know. But it did emerge, and is still emerging more and more; fir. probably in the dealing of man with man, then in the dealing of families with other families. In the dealing of tribes with tribes in prehistoric times, the question of right and wrong played probably little or no part; might alone settled matters. In what we call the pagan world, among the early Egyptians, Hebrews, Greeks, and Romans, the law of might in the dealings of one nation with another prevailed, and up to our own time the standard of international morality has been, and still is, far below the standard among individuals and neighborhood communities. Even in the United States there is a crying want of public conscience. The people are preyed upon by men they elect to serve them. The men or corporations that take pleasure and satisfaction in serving the public well and reasonably, or in giving a *quid pro quo*, are rare. Men who are blameless in their personal dealings with one another will, when formed into a board of directors or trustees, rob railroads, and squander money not their own. Capitalists will band together to rob the state through the construction of sham highways or flimsy public buildings. A public conscience is among all peoples of slow growth, and an international conscience is still slower. What part has it played in the history of Europe? Surely a very minor part. The Golden Rule has been turned into an iron rule of might over right times without number, by all the nations recently engaged in war?

As man's moral consciousness has developed, the

question of right and wrong has, of course, come more and more to the front; his relations to his fellows, his sense of justice, of truth, of fair dealing, have occupied him more and more. His savage instincts have been held more and more in check. The coöperation and sympathy and good-will which have brought about his present civilization would have been possible on no other terms. Without a sense of justice, of love of truth, of ideal right, where should we have been to-day? The fittest to survive among mankind were those races that had the moral consciousness most fully developed. This gave a might which led to a permanent supremacy — a beneficent might. A malevolent might is one that is founded upon superior brute or material strength alone. The law of the jungle or of the tornado or of the avalanche, introduced into human affairs and unchecked by the law of man's moral nature, leads to wars of conquest, as it did to the World War.

IV

THE expounders of the benefits of war write and speak about it as if it were some system of hygiene or medicine or gymnastic training that a people could practice in and of themselves; whereas wars of conquest do not begin and end at home. There are two parties to such a war. If it is a benefit to the victors, what is it to the defeated? I am speaking, of course, of material benefits. The benefits that come from heroism and self-denial are of another order. If the lamb inside the lion is a benefit to the lion, what is it to the lamb? If Germany reaped advantage by her invasion of Belgium, what did Belgium reap? But the fate of the other party is the last question that would ever occur to the Prussian military mind. If the doctrine of frightfulness began and ended at home, the world could not object. Because burned cities in modern times rise from their ashes in new beauty and power, shall we therefore seek to rejuvenate our cities by applying a match to them? Cities rise from their ashes because of their stored-up wealth and because of the arteries of commerce and industry that flow through them. Fire does not rejuvenate a dead tree nor a dead city, nor does war rejuvenate a people who are in a state of mortal ripening. It did not rejuvenate Rome in ancient times, nor Spain in modern times, and it does not appear to be rejuvenating Mexico very fast, nor any of the South American republics. All depends upon the stock you are trying to rejuvenate.

Lord Roberts is quoted as saying, just before his death, that war is necessary and salutary, and that it is the only national tonic that can be prescribed when peace begets degeneracy in an over-civilized people. He looked upon Germany as the greatest friend of the Allies when she declared war against them. But could there be any better proof that peace had not begotten degeneracy in England or France or Russia than the promptness with which these countries took up the challenge of Prussian militarism, and the fortitude and self-denial with which they gave it blow for blow?

Under the smiling face of peace, when the demand is made, the heroic element is always found to be slumbering. Every day, in the industrial and scientific fields, men prove themselves the same heroes that they do on the field of battle, and they prove it without the excitement and stimulus that war gives; and women prove it in times of peace and times of war.

The gospel of war as a national tonic in our time is a delusion and a snare. Are we to get up a war offhand because we think the nations need that kind of medicine? Blood-letting is a strange remedy for the depleted condition to which Lord Roberts refers. War sets up the victorious nation, but how about the defeated one? Have the defeats of Spain in the past two or three hundred years set her up? Have the defeats of Turkey redounded to her glory and power? Little doubt that this World War will bear fruit, but it will be a kind of fruit the combatant did not seek or expect.

The conclusion, then, that I arrive at is that a new rule of conduct for nations as for individuals, a new biological law, has come into being through man's moral nature, his sense of right and wrong. There is no question of right or of wrong in the world of living things below man, and we can persuade ourselves that there is only by putting ourselves in the place of the struggling animal forces. And there is no question of right and of wrong in the human world till man's consciousness of this difference has begun to dawn. In our day this consciousness is sufficiently developed to become the ruling factor in the conduct of national and international affairs, and must very soon put an end to all armed human conflicts. In saying this I am not exploiting a theory; I am trying to state an indisputable scientific fact.

X

TOOTH AND CLAW

I

TO deny that Nature is cruel, in the strict sense of the term, were, to the majority of persons, like denying that blood is red, or that fire will burn. We use the term "cruel" loosely, and interpret the ways of Nature in terms of our own psychology.

If we are torn by thorns or stung by nettles or bitten by snakes or suffer from frost-bites or sun-stroke, we accuse Nature of cruelty, always assuming, in our conceit, that we are the lords of creation, and that things were made especially for us. We have no venomous snake that will bite us except in self-defense, nor any bee that will sting us except on the same grounds.

Even Darwin, in a letter to his friend Hooker, refers to the "clumsy, wasteful, blundering, slow, and horribly cruel works of Nature," thus treating the All-Mother with scant respect.

Amiel cannot say, as he does say, that "Nature is unjust and shameless, without probity and without faith," unless he makes her over into man or invests her with the human consciousness. Even the good Emerson accuses Nature of being unscrupulous. Did the Concord philosopher expect storms and frost and blight and thunderbolts to have scruples? Did he expect thorns and nettles and fleas and potato-bugs and grasshoppers and disease-germs to consider their ways?

A well-known philosopher and writer, Professor Jacks, of Manchester College, Oxford, in writing upon "Our Common Foe," takes it for granted at the outset that Nature is cruel, and, moreover, that she is as cruel as the Germans showed themselves to be in the cruelest of all wars. "There is a cruelty in Nature," he says, "and it has been reserved for our age to realize how immense is its range and how appalling its effects"; we realize it, he says, when we read the story of Germany's treatment of her prisoners, the story of her submarines, and her conduct toward unoffending non-combatants generally.

What worse thing could be said about Nature than that she is as bad as the Germans? It almost makes us suspect treachery and death in her summer breezes and her sunshine. Dr. Jacks seeks to justify his charge by averring that man is a part of Nature and that in him are summarized her good and her evil qualities. Of course, in a certain sense this is true. But in seeking to solve the problems of his life, man separates himself from the rest of Nature and holds himself amenable to standards of conduct that he does not apply to the orders below him. He regards himself as a superior being. He is a part of Nature, but of an emancipated and regenerated Nature. He is one with the beasts of the field and the fowls of the air only in his purely animal aspects. As a moral and spiritual being with a sense of truth and justice, of mercy and forgiveness, he stands on a higher plane. He cannot justify his conduct by an appeal to brute nature or to biological laws. His sins are more scarlet and his virtues more divine than those of his unmoral and unreasoning brute neighbors. His consciousness of right and wrong is the touchstone by which all his deeds are to be tried.

Tennyson's agonizing line "Nature red in tooth and claw" tends, especially in the days of world-wide human carnage, to make one see the whole animal kingdom with blood-dripping claws and jaws. But it is not so. At its worst this "tooth and claw" business applies only to a fraction of wild life. The vast army of the seed-eaters, the plant-eaters, the fruit-eaters, upon which the flesh-eaters subsist, and which they help keep in check, is greatly in the ascendancy.

The whole truth of this matter of the cruelty of Nature may be put in a nutshell: Nature as seen in animal life is *sanguinary*, but only man is *cruel*. Only man deliberately and intentionally inflicts pain; only man tortures his victims, and takes pleasure in their agony. No other creature goes out of its way to inflict suffering; no other creature acts from the motive of cruelty or the will to give pain.

Nature kills, but does not torture. The biological laws are neither human nor inhuman; they are *un*-human. If in following the rule that might makes right, the Germans sought justification by an appeal to biological laws, they fell below the beasts of the fields, because they are moral beings, and know good from evil.

Biological laws are not concerned about the moral law. Not till we reach man's moral nature does this law have any validity; then it becomes a biological law, because it has survival value. Could the race of man ever have developed as we now see it without the conceptions of right and justice and the spirit of mutual helpfulness? As time passes, other things being equal, the most righteous and humanitarian nation will be the most powerful and the most progressive. The great strength of the Allied cause in the World War was that it was founded upon an ideal conception of international justice and comity. President Wilson set this forth in such wonderful completeness that it will shine in our political firmament for all time like a star of the first magnitude. And the weakness of the German cause was that it was based upon the spirit and the aims of the pirate and the highwayman.

When we speak of Nature's cruelty we are obsessed with the idea that blood and death necessarily mean cruelty, whereas cruelty, as I have said, means an intentional infliction of pain or suffering.

Is the surgeon cruel when he performs an operation? Do our own carnivorous habits imply cruelty? The slaughter-house is not a pleasant object to contemplate; the sight of blood disturbs most of us; its sight and smell excite even the unreasoning brutes. But it is the wanton shedding of blood that reacts unfavorably upon ourselves, and makes us indifferent to the suffering which blood so often implies. Life is a wonderful and precious gift, and we do not like to see it wantonly destroyed.

Professor Jacks speaks of "the hot, foul breath of Nature's cruelty," a sentence mild enough when applied to the Germans, but not justified when applied to universal Nature. We can hardly accuse the laws of matter and force of being cruel when they destroy us; if they were not true to themselves, what permanence would there be to life or to anything else? Fire and flood, the earthquake and the tornado, cause pain and death, gravity will crush us as soon as sustain us, but these forces are not cruel, because there is no will to inflict suffering; they are a part of the system of things upon which our life and well-being depend.

Nature, in the action of her mechanical and chemical forces as they go their way about us, is, as I have so often said, apparently as indifferent to man as to all other forms of life, but, to speak in the same terms of our human experience, something must have been solicitous about man or he would not be here in a world so well suited to his development and well-being. In the conflict of forces he has had to take his chances with other forms of life, but his powers of adaptation and invention far surpass those of all other creatures. Not an atom, not a pebble, will turn aside to save him from destruction. Unrelenting and unpitying Nature is the school in which his powers have been developed, and for him to call Nature "cruel" in her treatment of him is for a child to upbraid the parent whose guidance and discipline foster and safeguard the coming man. Could man have become man on any other terms?

Love is creation's final law, though Tennyson seems to doubt it when he sees Nature "red in tooth and claw." But tooth and claw do not necessarily imply cruelty, since the cruelest of all animals — man — has them not; they imply the dependence of one form of life upon another form, and are associated in our minds with that most heinous of all crimes, murder. It is Nature's seeming indifference to life which causes us to charge her with cruelty. Our minds can take in but a fraction of the total scheme of things, and what we do take in we make a personal application of to ourselves. We humanize when we should generalize.

The Germans willfully turned their backs upon the natural biological law of righteousness or rightness, and their punishment has been swift and adequate. They made a religion of cruelty, as man alone has exhibited it, and cultivated the will to destroy and defame till mankind, with one accord, bestowed upon them their ancestral name, the Huns. They went forth to burn and pillage and murder, and, so far as lay in their power, to destroy the very earth of the peoples they sought to conquer. They summoned to their aid all the diabolical forces of which chemistry is capable, and if they could have controlled the seismic and meteorological forces as well, who doubts that they would have made a desert, blackened with fire and torn by earthquakes, where dwell the nations that opposed them?

The spirit they showed in the World War, and the nefarious crimes of which they were guilty, make it a serious question whether or not they should not be forever cast out from the family of civilized nations; whether, indeed, they should not be completely wiped off the map as a nation, and their power for further evil forever destroyed.

"There is no place in the world of the future," says Dr. Jacks, "for a people whose policy is tainted by the instinct for cruelty."

If Nature were as cruel as the Germans are, if the same lust for blood and suffering had run in her veins, if she had, in the same spirit of riot and wantonness, destroyed her own creatures and laid waste her own provinces, would you or I, or any one else, have been here to pass judgment upon her doings?

TOOTH AND CLAW

There is blood and death in the jungle, but no lust of pain; but in the German prisons, and in the path of Germany's armies, there was the deliberate infliction of suffering and agony for their own sakes, so that for generations to come the name of Germany will stand for all that is selfish, cruel, unchivalrous, ignoble, insulting, and bestial in human history. The Prussian officer spat in the face of his prisoners of a like rank, and followed this with insulting epithets and blows, seeking in every way to bring them down to his own bestial level. The Prussian nurse brought to a wounded British soldier the glass of water he begged for, held it close to his face then poured it on the ground, handing him the empty glass. *These have since proved to be groundless accusations*

II

NATURE has an anæsthetic of her own which she uses in taking life. The carnivorous animals inflict far less pain than appearances would seem to indicate. Tooth and claw usually overwhelm by a sudden blow, and sudden blows benumb and paralyze. Violence in this light is the handmaiden of Mercy. If the surgeon could perform his operations in the same sudden and violent manner, an anæsthetic would rarely be needed. Livingstone was conscious of but little pain when in the jaws of a lion, and its prey no doubt feels as little. The human criminal, electrocuted or hung or beheaded, probably experi-

165

ences but little physical suffering. Any one whose life has been suddenly imperiled by a railway or a runaway accident knows how blessed is the blankness which comes over his mind at the most critical moment; the suddenness and intensity of his alarm blots out consciousness, and he retains no memory of just what happened. The soldier in battle may be seriously or fatally wounded and not be aware of it till some time afterward. A crushing or tearing blow disrupts the machinery of sensation. It is only when we put ourselves in the place of the mouse with which the cat is playing that we pity it; it does not experience the agony we should feel under like conditions; it is usually unwounded; it does not know what awaits it and its comparative freedom of movement soothes its alarm.

Dr. Jacks speaks of the bloody work of the struggle for existence, but the struggle for existence is largely a bloodless struggle of adaptation. Through it, every creature sooner or later finds its place, finds where it fits into the scheme of things. Through it the mouse finds its place, and the lion its, and man has found his. Living bodies are not ready-made, so to speak, like the parts of machinery; they are constantly in the making, and their making is a process of transformation. The horse, as we know him, was millions of years in the making; so was the elephant; so was man; so was every other form of life. The struggle for existence as a whole is cruel only so far as all discipline and all insensible modifications and adaptations under the pressure of environment are cruel; it is good in the guise of evil; it is the stern beneficence of impartial law. The greater the power of adaptation, the more fit is the animal or plant to survive, and this power of adaptation is mainly what distinguishes living bodies from non-living. Inanimate bodies tend to adjust themselves to one another through mechanical laws; animate bodies tend to adapt themselves to one another and to their environment through vital law.

The struggle for existence is for the most part a struggle with inanimate nature — with climate, soil, wind, flood. A peaceful struggle is going on all around us at all times, among men as among animals and plants: a struggle to live, to compel Nature to yield us the things needed for our lives. It is not often competition — an effort to win what another must lose; it is an effort to seize and appropriate the elements that all may have on equal terms, by the exercise of strength, industry, wit, prudence. Life is predaceous only to a limited extent. In the wilds, in the jungle, one form devours another form, but nature compensates. A fuller measure of life is given to those forms that are the prey of other forms; they are more prolific. The rats and mice are vastly more prolific than the weasels or the owls that feed upon them; the rabbits have ten young to one of their enemy, the fox; the lesser birds greatly outnumber the hawks; the little fishes that are the food of the big fishes swarm in the sea.

Probably no species is ever exterminated by its natural enemies. These enemies only keep it in check. The birds keep the insects from ruining vegetation, which is the source of all food. Slay all the lions in Africa, and probably the struggle for existence of the antelope tribe would soon be harder than it is now. Hence the animals of prey are a good gift even to the animals they prey upon. The plus of the breeding instinct of the latter would in time result in overpopulation and in famine.

The things that are preyed upon are more joyous and contented than their enemies. The carnivorous animals are solitary and morose; the birds of prey are the same. The chipmunk seems to have a much better time than the weasel, the bluebird than the owl that lines its nest with blue feathers. One might envy the song sparrow, or the vesper sparrow, or the robin, but never the shrike nor the sharp-skinned hawk that pursues them. The eagle is a grand bird, but evidently the lark is much the happier. The jay devours the eggs and the young of the smaller birds, but these birds greatly outstrip him in the race of life. The murderers evidently have less joy in their lives than the murdered. The crow rarely sheds blood, and, compared with the hawk, he is a happy-all-the-year-round vagabond.

Nature has made the wild creatures fearful of

their natural enemies, and has endowed them with means to escape them; then she has equipped these enemies with weapons and instincts to defeat this (her own) purpose. She plays one hand against another. Wild life is divided into two warring camps, and, as in our own wars, new devices for defense on the one hand are met with new devices of attack on the other. The little night rodents have big and sharp eyes, but the owl that preys upon them has big and sharp eyes also, and his flight is as silent as a shadow. You see, Nature is impartial; she has the good of all creatures at heart. If it is good for the hawk to eat the bird, it is good for the bird to be equipped with swift wings and sharp eyes to evade the hawk. A little more advantage on either side and the game would be blocked — the birds would fail or the hawks would starve. As it is, "the race is to the swift and the battle to the strong." Nature keeps the balance. Action and reaction are equal. The skunk and the porcupine have little or no fear; neither have they much wit. Their weapons of defense are nearly always ready, and that of the porcupine acts automatically; that of the skunk is a little more deliberate and inflicts less pain, but gives great discomfort and discomfiture.

Nature keeps one form in check with another form, and thus, like a wise capitalist, distributes her investments so that the income is constant. If she put her funds all in mice and birds, the cats and owls would soon starve; if she put them all in wood-chucks, the pastures and meadows would soon fail the herds. And this reminds me how man often disturbs the balance of nature; the clearing-up and the cultivation of the land have held in check the natural enemies of the woodchucks — foxes and owls — at the same time that they have greatly increased the woodchuck's sources of food-supply, so that in some sections these rodents have become a real pest to the farmer. The same changed conditions appreciably favor the meadow mice, and they, too, seem to be on the increase. But this increase again may stimulate the increase of the mice-hunting hawks, and thus the balance be maintained. Herein lies the danger of introducing new forms of wild life in a country — their natural enemies are not always on hand to check them. The mongoose has overrun Jamaica and has not yet found an adequate natural enemy. Introduced into this country, it would be an incalculable calamity, though in time it would doubtless meet with a natural check. Our weasels, related to the mongoose, are prolific, and seem to have few natural enemies, and yet they do not unduly increase; it seems as if some unknown hand must stay them. They prey upon all the smaller rodents and find them easy victims, yet these rodents are vastly more numerous than the blood-suckers. I often see marks upon the snow where the muskrat and the rabbit have fallen before them, and yet one sees scores of these animals to one weasel or mink.

How our domestic animals would suffer if they had the gift of ideation and knew what awaited them! Pope anticipated me when he wrote:

> "The lamb thy riot dooms to bleed to-day,
> Had he thy reason could he skip and play?
>
> "Pleased to the last he crops the flowery food,
> And licks the hand just raised to shed his blood."

If the horse only knew his own strength, and knew that he had "rights," would there not soon be a horse rebellion? Would the swine and the cattle fatten in their pens and stalls if they knew what is before them? Animals suffer no mental anguish either over the past or concerning the future; they live in the present moment; no future looms before them, no past haunts their memories. Their pain is brief, their joy is unconscious; they live to feed and breed; they slay without penalties, and they are slain without remorse; they find their place and live their day, and Mother Nature reaps the harvest.

Would we have a world without struggle or pain or friction of any kind? Good means ease, leisure, security; but it means something more: it means achievement, victory, the overcoming of evil, the development of power, the making of the world a better place to live in, and much more. Is Nature a tyrant because we have to earn our living? Because we have to plow and plant and hoe? Because flood and fire will destroy us, and the winds rack us, if we loose our grip? We have life on these terms; they are the conditions that beget and sustain life. A world void of evil, as we use the word, would be a world void of good also, a negative world. Without death there can be no life; without struggle there can be no power.

XI

MEN AND TREES

I DO not see that Nature is any more solicitous about the well-being of man than she is, say, about the well-being of trees. She is solicitous about the well-being of all life, so far as the conditions of life favor its development and continuance — men and trees alike. But all have to run the gantlet of some form of hostile forces — the trees one kind, man another. What I mean is that evil in some form waits upon all — hindrances, accidents, defeat, failure, death.

The trees and the forests have their enemies and accidents and set-backs, and men and communities of men have analogous evils. Trees are attacked by worms, blight, tornadoes, lightning, and men are attacked by pestilence, famine, wars, and all manner of diseases. Every tree struggles to stand upright; it is the easiest and only normal position. Men aspire to uprightness of thought and conduct, but a thousand accidental conditions prevent most of them from attaining it. One tree in falling is likely to bring down, or to mutilate, other trees, as the moral or business downfall of a strong man in a community is quite sure to bring evil to many others around him. Trees struggle with one another for moisture and sustenance from the soil, and for a place in the sun, as men do in the community, and the most lucky, or the most fit, survive. Nature plans for a perfect tree as she plans for a perfect man, but both tree and man have to take their chances with hostile forces and conditions amid which their lot falls, so that an absolutely perfect oak or elm or pine is about as rare as a perfect man. Of course Nature has endowed man with mental and spiritual powers which she has not bestowed upon trees. These powers give man an advantage over trees, but not the same advantage over men — his own kind of tree — because his fellows are similarly endowed. His struggle with his own kind is as inevitable as the struggle of trees with their kind, with this advantage in favor of the trees: theirs is always a peaceful competition, it never takes the form of destructive wars. Trees of opposite kinds will draw away from one another; a pine will draw away from a maple or an oak, not, I suppose, because of any natural antagonism, but because it is less mobile and its tender but more rigid branches cannot stand the buffetings of the more mobile and flexible deciduous trees. Pine loves to associate with pine, and spruce with spruce. The spirit, the atmosphere of a pine or a hemlock forest, how different from that of a beech or a maple! Most trees tend to associate themselves together in large bodies, as did primitive man, and civilized man, too, for that matter. The conifers are more clannish than the deciduous trees.

Are not a generation of leaves and a generation of men subject to about the same laws of chance? The baby leaves have their enemies in insects that devour them, in blight that withers them, in frost that cuts them short, and when they are matured, how the winds buffet them (Nature does n't temper the wind to the tender leaf), how the gales lash them, how the hail riddles them! If they had powers of thought, what a struggling, agitated, unstable world they would think themselves born into! When a summer tempest strikes a maple- or an oak-tree, the strain and stress of the foliage is almost painful to witness. Yet when the tempest subsides, hardly a leaf is torn or detached, and when autumn comes, the ranks of the vast army of the leaves are but little thinned, and the great majority of leaves ripen and fall to the ground unscathed. They have come through the campaign of life and have experienced many ups and downs, and yet, on the whole, they have each had an active and useful life. The leaf-rollers have made their nests in a few of certain kinds of them, the leaf-cutters have made holes in certain other kinds, the gall insects have made their nurseries at the expense of still other kinds; but all these things amount to a small fraction of the whole. When a plague of forest worms comes and strips the maples or the beeches, or a plague of elm-beetles strips the elms, and the invasion of a foreign deadly fungus kills all the chestnuts, these calamities are paralleled by the plagues that in past times have swept away large numbers of human beings and depopulated whole countries, or by epidemic diseases, such as infantile paralysis, that now and then rage over widespread areas.

Go and sit down in our mixed beech, maple, birch, and oak woods and witness the varying fortunes of the trees. How many of them have had misfortunes of one kind or another! How few, if any, have reached their ideal! How many are diseased or dying at the top or decaying at the root! Some have been mutilated by the fall of other trees. Youth and age meet and mingle. Some trees in their teens, as it were, are very thrifty; others are old and decrepit. In fact, the fortunes of the individual trees are much like those of men and women in a human community — struggle, competition, defeat, decay, and death on all sides. All, or nearly all, the evils that afflict men have their counterpart in the evils that afflict the trees of the forest. When some species of forest worm threatens the destruction of our beech or maple forests some other form of insect-life steps in and puts an end to their increase, and the plague vanishes. The gypsy and the brown-tailed moths which have so ravished the groves and forests of the Eastern States will doubtless in time be held in check by their natural enemies. The plague of tent

caterpillars that got such headway in New York
State that it threatened to become a public calamity
was effectually checked by the cold and rain of the
May of 1917. Not one tent caterpillar have I seen
during the past three years. The plague of currant-
worms was checked in the same way. Sooner or later
any excess is sure to be corrected. But so far as we
can see, such things as the chestnut blight and hick-
ory blight must rage like a fire till they have spent
themselves and there are no more chestnut- or hick-
ory-trees to be destroyed. Throughout the course of
the biological history of the globe, both plants and
animals have dropped out in some such way, and
new forms come in — come in through the slow action of the evolutionary impulse.

The Providence I see at work in the case of the
trees does not differ at all from the Providence I see
at work in the case of men. It is one and the same,
and that one is as I have so often said, wholesale,
indiscriminating, regardless of individuals, regardless of waste, delays, pain, suffering, failure, yet in-
suring success on a universal scale, the scale of centuries and geologic periods. Our standards of time
compared with Nature's standards are like our in-
terplanetary spaces compared with the inconceivable abysses of the sidereal heavens — minutes compared to centuries. Our little family of planets
moves round the fireside of our little sun — a
small chimney-corner in the vast out-of-doors of

astronomic space, where suns and systems and whole universes of worlds drift like bubbles on the sea. Give Nature time enough, and the world of to-day, or of any day, becomes an entire stranger to you. Orion will no longer stalk across the winter skies, the pole-star will no longer guide your ships, if, indeed, there remains any ocean for your ships to sail upon.

The Natural Providence is not concerned about you and me. In comparison it is concerned only about our race, and not lastingly concerned about that, since races, too, shall go.

> "Races rise and fall,
>   Nations come and go;
> Time doth gently cover all
>   With violets and with snow."

As I sit here under an old heavy-topped apple-tree on a hot midsummer day, a yellow leaf lets go its hold upon the branch over my head and comes softly down upon the open book I am reading. It is a perfect leaf, but it has had its day. The huge family of leaves of which it was a member are still rank and green and active in sustaining the life of the tree, but this one has dropped out of the leafy ranks. There are a few small dark spots upon it, which, I see with my pocket glass, are fungus growths, or else some germ disease of apple-tree leaves, perhaps, like pneumonia, or diphtheria, or tuberculosis among men. One leaf out of ten thousand has fallen.

Was Fate cruel to it? From the point of view of the leaf, yes — could a leaf have a point of view; from the point of view of Nature, no. The tree has leaves enough left to manufacture the needed chlorophyl, and that satisfies the law. If all the leaves were blighted, or were swept off by insect enemies, or stripped by hail and storm, that were a calamity to the tree. But one leaf, though all the myriad forces of Nature went to its production, though it is a marvel of delicate structure and function, though the sun's rays have beaten upon it and used it, and been kind to it, though evolution worked for untold ages to bring its kind to perfection — what matters it? It will go back into the soil and the air from which it came, and contribute its mite to another crop of leaves, and maybe it has rendered the molecules of carbon and hydrogen and oxygen of which it is composed more ready and willing to enter into other living combinations. And the fungus germs that have preyed upon it, they, too, have had their period of activity, and have justified themselves. Nature thus pits one form against another, and her great drama of life and death goes on. Are her stakes more in the one than in the other, since she favors both? Yes, she has more at stake in health than in disease. If disease always triumphed, all life would go out. Of course, in the sum total of things, the life of this old tree counts for but little, but if it failed to bear apples, its chief end would be defeated. Evil is limited; it is a minor counter-current, but it is just as real as the good; it is a phase of the good; we have evil because we first have good. Both are relative terms. We are prone to speak of good and evil as if they were something absolute, like gravity or chemical affinity. But are they any more absolute than heat and cold, or than big and little? What pleases us, and is conducive to our well-being, we call good, and its opposite we call evil. We are not to make our wants and dislikes, our pleasures and our pain, the measure of the universe, as we do mathematics and physics. We can think of things in terms of art and literature, of beauty or ugliness, or in terms of morality and religion, or we may think of them in terms of science and of exact knowledge. When we say they are good or bad, we are thinking of them in terms of morals or of religion; when we say they are beautiful or ugly, we are describing them in terms of æsthetics; when we say they are true or false, real or delusive, we are talking of them in terms of science.

This sere and prematurely ripened leaf appeals to my literary and imaginative faculties through its beauty and its symbolic character; it appeals to my understanding, my love of accurate knowledge, by reason of the blight that caused its fall.

Our going out of the world seems equally fortuitous and haphazard in infancy, youth, middle life, old age; before we have fairly lived, or after life has

lost its value, or in the height of our powers, or in
the decrepitude of old age: which shall it be?

The naturist sees all life as a whole. Man is not an
exception, but part of the total scheme. The life
principle is the same in him as in all else below him
— the principle that organizes matter into countless new forms; that crosses and uses the mechanical
and chemical forces, and begets numberless new
compounds; that develops organs and functions,
and separates the living world so sharply from the
non-living. In the weed, the tree, and in man, the
principle is the same. What has set up this organizing power and so impressed it that it goes on from
lower to higher forms, and unfolds the whole drama
of evolution through the geologic ages, is the mystery of mysteries. To solve this mystery, mankind
invented God and acts of creation. But a God apart
from Nature is to me unthinkable, and science finds
no beginning of anything. It finds change, transformation, only. When or where did man begin?
Where does the circle begin? Self-beginning — who
can think of that? Can we think of a stick with only
one end? We can think of a motion as beginning and
ending, but not of substance as beginning and ending. When the metabolism of the body ceases, death
comes. Do we think of life, or the organizing principle, as then leaving the body? It ceases, but does it
leave the body in any other sense than that the
flame leaves the candle when it is blown out? And is

this any different in the case of man than it is in the case of a tree or a dog? We postulate what we call a soul in man, which we deny to all other forms of life — an independent entity which separates from the body and lives after it. But we run into difficulties the moment we do so. In the biologic history of man, when and where did the soul appear? Did the men of the old Stone Age, of whom Professor Osborn writes so graphically and convincingly, have it? Did the Piltdown man, the Neanderthal man, the Java man of Du Bois, have it? Did our ancestral forms still lower down have it? Do babies have it? Do idiots and half-witted persons have it?

All we can claim for man above the lower orders is higher intelligence, greater brain power, the power of reflection, and the logical process. His dog has perceptive intelligence, but not reflective; animals act from inherited impulse; man from impulse, thought, ideation. Man's instinctive impulses are guided or restrained by thought; his emotions — anger, love — wait upon thought; his migratory instinct waits as that of the lower animals does not. But when this extra power began, who can say? It had no beginning, it dawned by insensible degrees, as do all things in Nature. We have only to heighten our conception of Nature and matter to see the difficulties vanish — and the stigma of materialism loses its terrors.

In these later centuries mankind has steadily

grown bolder and bolder in dealing with its deities
and its devils. A few heroic spirits have always
questioned the truth of the popular creeds, but in
our day a very large majority question or even deny
them. Fear of the wrath above or the wrath below
has fled. Men are fast coming to see that devotion
to the truth is the essence of true religion, and that
the worst form of irreligion is the acceptance of
creeds and forms without examining them, or upon
the sole authority of some book or sect. The truth-
loving man is the God-loving man. We no longer
talk of God-fearing men — this negative attitude
has given place to the positive attitude of love and
enjoyment. The wrath of God no longer makes us
tremble. The swift and sure vengeance of violated
law, both in the physical world without us and the
physiological world within us, we understand and
appreciate, but the fury and revenge of the offended
gods no longer disturb our dreams. Nature has no
mercy, is no respecter of persons, is one to the just
and the unjust. Only the moral nature of man
knows right from wrong; only the reason of man
knows truth from falsehood. When or how man got
this moral and intellectual nature is a question upon
which men themselves will never agree. Did it come
from without or from within — through evolution
or revelation? The naturalist or naturist is bound to
believe that it came from within through the long
process of evolution. Whatever favored man's de-

velopment became a biological law and had survival value. Without some degree of right conduct and fair dealing — some degree of perception of the true and the false — the race of man could never have attained its present high position in the scale of animate nature. Through some inherent impulse or tendency in matter, man arose out of the earth, climbing through the many lowly forms to his full estate of a rational being. It has been a long and toilsome and painful journey. But here we are, and when we look back through the geologic vistas we are incredulous that we came that road. We incline to the short cut through the Garden. But the study of the ways of Nature as we see them in all living things opens our eyes to the truth of evolution. Of course the great puzzle and mystery is, Who or what stamped upon matter this organizing and developing impulse and caused the first unicellular life in the old Azoic or Palæozoic seas to branch and grow and increase in complexity till it gave birth to all the myriad living forms, high and low, that now fill the earth? But here again I am using the language of half-truth — the language of our experience, which makes us think of some external agent as stamping an impulse upon matter. If we say the impulse was always there, that it is inseparable from matter and the laws of matter, just as creation is without beginning and end, center or circumference, we come no nearer speaking the unspeakable. But it seems to me we do, in a measure, satisfy the reason; we make it see or realize its own limitations; reason guides reason.

The infinite knows neither time nor space, neither extension nor duration; it knows only the here and the now. It does not wait for time to pass or for eternity to begin. Eternity is now. Man, and all that has arisen out of him, is a part of universal nature. Are we not held to the sphere? Can we disturb it in its orbit? Can we banish one atom from it or add one atom to it? We are a fragment of it, its laws pervade our minds, and we cannot get away from the necessity of putting our thoughts and emotions in the terms of our experience as dwellers upon this astronomic globe. We may fancy that we get away from it in moments of abstract thought, but we do not; we do not get away from ourselves any more than we can outrun our shadow. We can let our imaginations course with the spheres that circle through the abysmal depths of space, but we can put our emotions only in the words that we have invented to describe our experiences in this little three-dimensional corner of creation. If our terms were formed from our experiences amid the spheres, we might be able to give some hint of the Infinite. We might learn how to describe our sensations when emancipated from the standards and limitations of the world in which we live.

Conventionally religious persons shrink from

having their spiritual life discussed in terms of psychology, because psychology smacks of science and science acts like a blight upon religion. It dispels mystery and lets the light of day — the garish, irreligious day — into the twilight or the darkness of religious emotion. We do not want our relation to the spiritual world explained in terms of our common knowledge — such is our hankering after the unknown, the mysterious, the transcendent.

One side of our nature fears the Infinite, and we experience a chill when the methods of this world obtrude themselves there. We have convinced ourselves that the part of our inner life which we call the soul is something more sacred and mysterious and nearer to the Infinite than our ordinary faculties. What victims we are of words! What is the value of this feeling, and how did it arise? Our appreciation of the beautiful, in art and nature, is equally extra and transcends our practical faculties. Man's belief in another world — an ideal world of the absolute good — is, of course, the result of his strong reaction from the pain, the struggle, the incompleteness of this world. Evolution is a hard road to travel. Being born is evidently not a pleasant experience for the baby, and in this world man is constantly struggling through new experiences into a higher and larger life. His measure of happiness is never full and he looks for compensation in another and better world. He does not see that there can be no better world — that pain and struggle and disappointment are necessary for his development, and that to long for a state in which these things do not exist is like the stream longing for a dead equilibrium. All power and all growth come from a break in the repose of the physical forces. There is no power in a uniform temperature, nor in water at a dead level. Mechanical power comes down an incline, vital power is a lift on an up-grade — all growing things struggle upward; the vegetable and animal world lift the earth elements up against gravity into an unstable equilibrium. Mechanical things run down the scale toward a stable equilibrium.

Our life goes on by virtue of some principle or force in matter that tends constantly to break up the stable into the unstable, to force the elements into new chemical combinations. Our machines dissipate energy in doing work; the living body conserves energy in the same process. It grows strong by the obstacles it overcomes, up to the limits of its powers. The clock runs down, the energy we put into it in winding it up is dissipated; but the growth of a living body is a winding-up process, a drawing-in and a storing-up process. In the wood and coal we burn is stored up the heat of the sun. In burning them and driving machinery by means of the heat developed, the energy is dissipated. In manual labor the human body dissipates energy also, and it is the same solar energy that the engine dissipates, and it does it in the same mechanical way; and it is constantly replenished from without through the food consumed. But the human or living engine stokes itself. It is a clock that winds itself up, a gun that loads and points itself. Because the living body in its final analysis turns out to be a machine as absolutely dependent upon mechanical and chemical principles as any other machine, there are those who see no radical difference between the mechanical and the vital.

I conclude that it is equally up-grade from the vital or physiological to the psychical. How the two connect we can never know, but that the thinking man dissipates energy there is no doubt. The body and the soul are one in a way past our finding out. When we discuss these things in terms of metaphysics, we launch upon a boundless sea and reach no real port.

When we project ourselves into Nature out of which we came, or when we see ourselves there objectively,— our virtues, our aspirations, our vices, and our wickedness,—we sow the seeds of our religion. We grow a crop of gods and of devils, and heaven and hell become fixed realities to us. So do we make the world in which we live, and it in turn makes us. So does the divine in us keep pace with the divine we see in Nature. So does the beauty of our own characters grow as we see beauty in the character of others. So do our love, faith, hope, charity, develop and augment as we see these things in the world about us. The universe is thus constituted, and that is all we can say about it.

That right, human right, in the end and on a large scale, prevails, I believe to be true; the right that in long periods of time means, or rather secures, the well-being of the race — the greatest good to the greatest number.

In discussing the final problems of the universe, we are attempting to describe the Infinite in terms of the finite — an impossible task. We think and speak of God as a person, because our experience gives us no other terms in which to conceive Him except in terms of personality. He sees, hears, plans, governs, creates, loves, suffers, is angry, we say, — in fact, has all human attributes and characteristics vastly magnified. He is an omnipotent and omnipresent man. He is the creator and organizer and director of the universe, and hence is responsible for everything in it, the evil as well as the good. Our attitude toward Him is that of a subject toward his sovereign, or toward a supreme judge. We must praise, exalt, supplicate, propitiate Him. There is lying upon my table a recent volume of sermons by an English divine called "The Justification of God" — his justification in the face of the terrible World War which he might have prevented. Thus, just as soon as we conceive of God in terms of our human nature, these baffling problems thrust themselves upon us. We must seek some grounds upon which we can excuse or vindicate or justify this supreme man for permitting the terrible happenings which darken the world. As this is not an easy task, men say in their hearts, and often with their lips: "There is no God." Better no God than a being who would permit the sin and suffering we see daily all about us, and that history reveals to us.

The only alternative I see is to conceive of God in terms of universal Nature — a nature God in whom we really live and move and have our being, with whom our relation is as intimate and constant as that of the babe in its mother's womb, or the apple upon the bough. This is the God that science and reason reveal to us — the God we touch with our hands, see with our eyes, hear with our ears, and from whom there is no escape — a God whom we serve and please by works and not by words, whose worship is deeds, and whose justification is in adjusting ourselves to his laws and availing ourselves of his bounty, a God who is indeed from everlasting to everlasting. Of course in the light of the old theology this is no God at all. It was to emancipate us from the rule of this God that the old conceptions of a being above and far removed from Nature were formulated. Nature is carnal and unholy. Our theory compels us to say to matter and the laws of

matter, "Get thee behind me, Satan." We struggle
and suffer in this debasing world for a season, and
then escape from it to a higher and better one. In
all the dark, prescientific ages during our own era
— dark in regard to man's real relation to the
universe in which he finds himself, but often luminous with flashes of insight into the nature of man
himself — these conceptions ruled man's religious
aspirations. In our own times they still largely rule
in various modified forms. The old theological
dogmas are more or less discredited, but a religion
founded upon science makes little headway with
the average man. We are shaping our practical
lives — our business, our social, our economical
relations, more and more according to scientific
deductions. We seek more and more a scientific or
naturalistic basis for our rules of conduct, for our
altruism, for our charitable organizations, for our
whole ethical system. Any principle that squares
with natural law is indeed founded upon a rock.
The stars in their courses fight for the cause that is
founded upon natural right, which in human relations does not mean the right of the strong to
trample upon the weak, but the right of all to their
full measure of free development.

Right and wrong are, of course, finite terms, and
apply only in the human sphere. Universal Nature,
as it appears among non-living bodies and forces,
knows neither right nor wrong; it knows only

might. As it appears among the orders below man, it knows neither right nor wrong. Physics and chemistry have no consciousness; neither have beasts or bacteria; but man has, and this fact will in time determine the whole course of human history. Naturalism makes for righteousness, or right-mindedness, as surely as it makes for health and longevity.

XII

THE PROBLEM OF EVIL

I

HOW has the problem of evil tried men's souls! How have their gods failed to live up to the character they have given them! How have they confused our moral standards! The trouble lies in a misconception of the nature of evil, and in a false idea of the universe itself.

There is no problem of evil until we have made or imagined an unnatural and impossible world. When we have enthroned in the universe a powerful man-made God who is the embodiment of all we call good and the contemner of all we call evil, then we have our insoluble problem. To help ourselves out we invent another being who is the embodiment of all we call evil and enthrone him in regions below. Upon him we saddle the evil, and thus we try to run the universe with these two antagonistic principles yoked together, and no end of confusion in our religious ideas results.

The moment we postulate an all-loving, all-merciful, all-wise, and just being to rule the affairs of this world, and place him in such intimate relations with it that not a sparrow falls to the ground without his will and cognizance, then, indeed, are we in troubled waters and have lost our reckoning. We cannot excuse such being on the ground that his ways are inscrutable and past finding out. A creator who sends into the world the malformed, the half-witted, the bestial, the naturally depraved, and then holds them to high ethical standards, is condemned by the ideals which he has implanted within us.

Now the naturalist has no such trouble. He sees that good and evil are only relative terms; that they both grow on the same tree; that we should not know good were there no evil; that there would be no development were there not what we call evil. Pain and suffering are inseparable from the human lot. They are a part of the price we pay for our place in the world. All struggle we look upon as evil. Disease, failure, death are looked upon as evil, but they are conditions of our lives. Through sickness we learn the laws of health. The lower animals have no such troubles — no sickness, intemperance, or war or avarice. They know without reason how to live, but man has reason, and the joy of its exercise and the peril of its failure. Are we not all willing to pay the price? — to take it on these terms rather than to change places with the brutes?

What a troublesome time the good orthodox brethren have with their God! He does, or permits such terrible things. Only yesterday He sent a cyclone through the State of Illinois that killed hundreds of innocent persons, and destroyed hundreds of peaceful homes, wiping out at one blow the results of long years of human labor. A few years ago He sent or permitted the scourge of infantile paralysis that desolated tens of thousands of homes and left a trail of thousands of crippled and enfeebled children. Again He sent or permitted the influenza to sweep over the land, claiming more victims than did the Great War; and so on. How our fathers, rocked in the cradle of the old creeds, wrestled with this problem! How could a paternal and all-loving God do these things? The naturalist reads nature differently. His god is no better than Nature. In fact, his god and Nature are one and inseparable. Nature goes her way and her ways are not our ways. We take our chances in the clash and war of physical forces. They have developed us and made us what we are.

It was only a few years ago that the President of the United States asked all good people to assemble in their respective places of worship and pray to God to stop the tornado of war and crime that was then devastating Europe. Is it possible to conceive of a being anywhere in the universe, with power to stop such a world calamity, who would complacently look on and wait till the sufferers could unite in a petition to him? What a false man-made god such a conception holds up to us! No wonder the

World War shattered this conception in thousands of minds, and left them without any faith at all!

Rogers said in regard to evil that Sir John Mackintosh and Malthus and another philosopher whose name has escaped me, all agreed that the attributes of the deity must be in some respects limited, else there would be no sin and misery in the world.

We use the words "good" and "evil" in a narrow, personal sense. To the farmer the frost that blights his crops is an evil, but not to the squirrels who are waiting for the nuts to fall, or to the man who suffers from hay fever. Rain is a blessing, but how easily it becomes a curse! A cold wet spring cuts off the insect pests, but delays the plowing and planting. It is hard on the insectivorous birds, but the plants and trees profit. The grasshoppers that eat up the farmer's pasturage make good provender for his flock of turkeys.

Blight and struggle, frost and drought, weed out the weaklings and beget a hardier race.

Moral evil — intemperance, avarice, war, lying, cheating — are on another plane. They are peculiar to man. Nature below him knows them not. But as they are against nature, they perpetually tend to correct themselves. The business world has learned that honesty is the best policy. Cheating is unpopular because, in the long run, it does not pay.

The most aggressive and warlike nation upon the

globe has at last got its eyes open to the evils of militarism, and has bought its emancipation at a heavy price. Tyranny and oppression are finally doomed by the nature of man. Nature's ways are roundabout, and often regardless of cost. The chaos and waste and suffering in Europe to-day are in keeping with her spendthrift methods. She knows that the most turbulent and muddy stream will clear itself and quiet down. The track of the cyclone through the forest will in time entirely disappear. Evil perishes, the good increases more and more. God is not so bad as we paint him, and we have no need of a devil. All is good. Gravity would glue our feet to the ground and we have to defeat it every time we lift a foot, and yet how could we walk or work without gravity? The bad, or the evil, dogs one's footsteps, but it teaches us circumspection, and to beware of dangerous paths.

How easy to put one's finger on this or that and say, "Here are positive evils!" — all diseases, smallpox, infantile paralysis, influenza, and so on — but they are only remote contingencies, and, on the whole, most of us find life good. There are good germs and there are bad germs, but the good vastly predominate. And the bad germs are only bad from our point of view. Our doors and windows let in the cold or the heat, as the case may be. We have them on these conditions. Fruits and grains nourish us, but they may injure us also.

ACCEPTING THE UNIVERSE

In 1916 my naturalist's faith prompted me to write thus of the World War: Two world forces are at death grips in this war. In terms of government it is autocracy against democracy; in terms of biology it is the unfit against the fit; in terms of man's moral nature it is might against right. Whatever triumph Prussian aggressiveness and ruthlessness may meet with, they must in time meet with defeat, else Evolution has miscarried, and its latest and highest product, man's moral nature, is, in its survival value, but dust and ashes.

II

THERE is positive good and there is negative good. We may say of health that it is a positive good, and of sickness that it is a negative good, because it reveals to us the conditions of health. In disease the body is struggling to regain its health — to recover and retain its normal condition. Its well-being is the result of a certain balance between contending forces. What we call the hostile forces appear only as the result of wrong living. The lower animals have none of our distempers because they live according to nature. Cattle do not get rheumatism by lying upon the wet, cold ground, nor pneumonia from exposure to cold and storm. In the freedom of the fields and woods it is quite certain that they would never become infected with tuberculosis. I doubt if the wild dog or the wolf ever have dog distemper, or if wild horses ever have crib-bite. Disease, as we know it, is a product of civilization.

Death, of course, is not an evil when it comes in the regular course of nature; it is an evil when it comes prematurely. The various social evils tend to correct themselves. Moral evils — lying, cheating, selfishness, uncharitableness — also tend to correct themselves. Righteousness exalteth a nation because righteousness has great survival value. The unrighteousness of Germany caused her final downfall. In an earlier age, when ethical standards were lower, she might have succeeded in dominating Europe. Our susceptibility to pain is not an evil inasmuch as it safeguards us against a thousand dangers. What I would say in a score of ways is that there is no evil in the human world not of our own making. Plagues and famines are always the result of human folly or short-sightedness. Filth breeds disease. Typhoid fever is a filth disease and is preventable. There is no god to blame for our distempers. Nature's hands are clean. The wind is never tempered to the shorn lamb, in spite of the proverb, but the shorn lamb has not been fleeced by Nature. A heavy snowfall is an evil in towns and cities, but a good thing for the country. It enables the meadow mice to girdle the apple-trees, but it is a coverlid that greatly profits the meadows themselves. It is therefore good to both mice and meadows.

Our greatest philosopher, William James, had a wide grasp of fundamental questions, but it seems to me that he did not fully grasp the problem of evil; he saw the universe as a dual universe, two principles, good and evil, struggling with each other. He seemed to look upon good and evil as positive entities in themselves, whereas naturalism sees in them only names which we give to our experiences with objects and conditions in this world. What favors us, as I have so often said, we call good, and what antagonizes we call evil; but absolute good and absolute evil do not exist, any more than do absolute up and down; or absolute near and far. The absolute admits of no degrees, but there are all degrees of good and bad. Some hostile germs are worse than others, and some friendly germs are better than others. Again I say, we live in a world of relativity.

Naturalism does not see two immeasurable realities, God and Nature, it sees only one, that all is Nature or all is God, just as you prefer.

James was fond of quoting Walt Whitman, but he does not see, as Whitman did, that there is no evil, or, if there is, that it is just as necessary as the so-called good. From James's point of view Nature is a harlot to whom we owe no allegiance, and another world is demanded to correct and compensate the failures and disappointments of this.

Our sacred books and traditions tell us of one God

who made the heaven and the earth, and who on looking upon them said that they were very good. Here is where the trouble begins — a Creator apart from the universe who looks upon and approves the work of his hands. This is the early, childish view of mankind. As Bergson says, when we apply to the universe our idea of a maker and a thing made, trouble begins. The universe was not made; it *is*, and always has been. God is Nature, and Nature is God. If this is pantheism, then we are in good company, for Goethe said that as a philosopher he was a pantheist. Even the atheist has a god of his own. He knows that there is something back of him greater than he is.

Most persons are pantheists without knowing it. Ask any of the good orthodox folk what God is, and they will say that He is a spirit. Ask them where He is, and they will answer, He is here, there, everywhere, in you and in me. And this is pantheism — all god — cosmotheism.

"Truly all that we know of good and duty proceeds from Nature; but, none the less so, all that we know of evil."

"If there be a divine spirit of the universe, Nature, such as we know her, cannot possibly be its ultimate word to man," says James. But does he not see that this term "divine spirit" is born of man's narrowness and partiality; that Nature is all of one stuff, divine or diabolical, just as we elect?

He says that the naturalistic superstition, the worship of God in nature, has begun to lose its hold upon the educated mind; that the first step toward getting into healthy relations with the universe is the act of rebellion against the God of nature.

Poor James Thomson, the British poet whose pessimism, perhaps, caused him to commit suicide, whom our James loves to quote, hurled his scorn at a fiction of his own brain when he wrote:

> "Not for all thy power, furled or unfurled,
>   For all thy temples to thy glory built,
>   Would I assume the ignominious guilt
> Of having made such men in such a world."

The whole value of philosophy is to help us to a rational view of the universe, and when it fails to do this, it falls short of fulfilling its proper function. The contradictions of which James speaks do not disturb the naturalist at all. Nature would not be Nature without these contradictions; they do not disturb the unity of Nature.

Empedocles taught that "there is no real creation or annihilation in the universal round of things, but an eternal mixing — due to the two eternal powers, Love and Hate — of one world-stuff in its sum unalterable and eternal." And Whitman's large lines mean the same thing:

> "There was never any more inception than there is now,
>   Nor any more youth or age than there is now,
>   And will never be any more perfection than there is now,
> Nor any more heaven or hell than there is now."

XIII

HORIZON LINES

I. THE ORIGIN OF LIFE

IN dealing with fundamental questions like the origin of life, how prone our natural philosophers are to assume the existence of that which they set out to prove. Thus Pflügler assumes *living* protein in the shape of a cyanogen radical, and assumes that this radical possesses a large amount of internal energy, and thus "introduces into the *living* matter energetic internal motion." As cyanogen and its compounds arise only in incandescent heat, he concludes that life is derived from fire, that its germ was in the earth when it was still an incandescent ball.

"As soon as oxides can be there," says Moore, "oxides appear." "When temperature admits of carbonates, then carbonates are forthwith formed." But are oxides and carbonates mere fortuitous compounds — just chance hits? Moore helps himself out by formulating what he calls the "Law of Complexity," a law that holds throughout all space. But is the law, again, fortuitous? Is it not rather organized intelligence? "Atoms, molecules, colloids, and living organisms arise as a result of the operation of this law." Allen says, "Life arose at the period when the physical conditions of the earth came to be nearly what they are at present." Of course. But is not this begging the question? We do not know life apart from these conditions; hence we assume that the conditions beget the life.

What is life anyhow? May we not say that it is a new motion in matter? It does not introduce a new chemistry, or a new physics, but it uses these to new ends. New and unstable compounds arise. Solar energy, says Allen, acting on various carbon and nitrogen compounds, would set up various anabolic and catabolic reactions which resulted in life — life of a very humble and rudimentary form, but life.

Troland gets life from the enzymes, but how does he get his enzymes? He assumes that at some moment in the earth's history a small amount of a certain autocatalytic enzyme — a self-created enzyme — suddenly appeared at a definite time and place within the yet warm ocean waters which contained in solution various substances reacting very slowly to produce an oily liquid immiscible with water. Troland postulates the auto- or self-catalytic character of the initial enzyme, which is virtually postulating the life-impulse itself.

Osborn, in his work on the "Origin and Evolution of Life," also virtually starts by assuming that which he sets out to prove. He suggests that the initial step in the origin of life was the coördinating and bringing together of the then primordial elements of water, nitrates, and carbon dioxide, "which so far as we know had never been in combined action before." Was their coming together a blind, fortuitous affair? Osborn assumes that these elements were gradually bound by a *new* form of mutual attraction "out of which arose a new form of unity in the cosmos, an organic unity or organism. It was an application of energy new to the cosmos. In fact it was life." "When the earth had in the course of its physical evolution become adapted as the abode of life, living substances came into being." By their own independent action, or by what?

In trying to account for happenings on the earth's surface, we follow the chain of cause and effect. But when we try to explain origins, we are dealing with a chain which has only one end.

Picted, a Swiss scientist, concluded that because all chemical action of the kind which goes on in living things is annihilated at one hundred degrees below zero Centigrade, therefore chemical action and life are one. But chemical action is as old as the earth. Is life as old?

II. THE LIVING AND NON-LIVING WORLDS

I FANCY I am not alone in having difficulty in uniting the two worlds — the living and the non-living — and in seeing them under the same law. In the one I see something like mind and purpose; every living thing shows something for which we have no name but intelligence. Organization demands an organizing principle. There is purpose in the wings of a bird, the legs of an animal, the fins of a fish, but where is there purpose in the orbs, in the comets, in the meteors? Or, to come down to the earth, where is there purpose in the mountains, in the stratified rocks, in the ocean, or in the air currents?

In a living body there are organs which function; in a non-living, there are parts which act and are acted upon. To see mind in all is the task — to see in gravity, in cohesion, in chemical affinity, in dissolution, anything at work akin to ourselves. We see irrefragable law; we see the sequence of cause and effect; we see the weather system work itself out — evaporation, condensation, precipitation, resulting in clouds, rainfall, springs, streams, lakes, and seas; we see the never-failing succession of the seasons; we see the law of the conservation of force; but do all these things imply the same intelligence, though unconscious, which we see in the sitting bird, or in the growing plant or tree? Is the cosmic order akin to the vital order? Of course mechanics and chemistry are one the universe over; atoms and molecules are atoms and molecules; but where does mind end, and law begin? Or, is it all law, or all mind, according to our point of view? The moral order, which is man's order, we know has its limits, but I am trying to see if the rational order is coexistent with nature. The unity we seek we may find in the old conception of God, but this saddles all the turmoil and disorder and evil of the world upon an all-wise, all-good Being.

Shall we adopt the idea of a primal mind as distinct from the human mind, as the poets do? I grasp at anything that will help me see that I am akin to the farthest star, in my mind as in my body. I cannot think of a dual or a divided universe. I want to see myself as strung upon the same thread as all the rest of nature.

In organic evolution I see the workings of the creative impulse — or growth, as opposed to mere accretion or accumulation. In the light of the same law does one not see worlds and suns potential in the spiral nebulæ? Science helps us to see the evolution of the chemical elements, or to follow up this defining and differentiating process. Could we fly to the uttermost parts of the heavens, we should find the Cosmic Mind there before us.

III. THE ORGANIZING TENDENCY

Is it possible to think of any ingenious contrivance in nature as the result of chance, or of the fortuitous clashing and jostling of the elements? Living things are full of these ingenious contrivances which serve a definite end and keep life going. In the inorganic world there are no such contrivances; there is not

the simplest bit of machinery — parts adjusted
to parts, and the whole adjusted to some specific
end. In all the clashing and jostling of bodies and
forces through all the astronomic and geologic
ages, not so much as the simplest mechanical de-
vice — a coiled spring or a carpenter's hammer
— has been struck out, and never can be. It is true
that there are certain static conditions of matter that suggest design — natural bridges, natural
obelisks, rude architectural and monumental struc-
tures, and human profiles on the rocks; but these
are not the result of a constructive process, of a
building-up, but the result of degradation: the ero-
sive forces carve them out in obedience to the laws
of matter and energy. We easily see how it all came
about; and we can guide these forces so that they
will repeat the process. But we do not see how the
living body, with all its marvelous adjustments and
coördinations, came about, and we cannot manipu-
late matter so as to produce the simplest living
thing. Darwinians profess to see in natural selection — which is simply a name for an eliminating or
sifting process — the explanation of even man himself. But the elimination of the weaker forms, which
has gone on for whole geologic ages — for example,
in the Grand Cañon of the Colorado — has not
resulted in so much as one perfect, four-square
foundation, or one perfect flying arch. Natural selection is not a creative, but a purely mechanical,

process. We involuntarily personify it, and think of it as involving will and power of choice; think of it as selecting this and that, as a man does when he weeds his garden or selects his seeds, or breeds his animals. But it is not positive at all. It is negative — a dropping-out process.

Chance, or chance selection, works alike in the organic and the inorganic realms, but it develops no new forms in the inorganic, because there is no principle of development, no organizing push. But in organized matter there is, in and behind all this organizing, a developing principle or tendency; the living force is striving toward other forms; in other words, development occurs because there is something to develop. An acorn develops, but a quartz pebble only changes.

The living body is placed in a world of non-living bodies and forces, and it takes its chances; it develops only by their aid; if warmth and moisture are withheld, it ceases to develop; or, if warmth and moisture are in excess, it ceases to develop; its well-being is insured when it rides the inorganic forces, and is not ridden by them. It is subject to the law of chance of the world in which it is placed, but that law of chance does not explain its origin or its development as it does that of the non-living forms.

That it is all the result of design or purpose of an all-wise Being, working his will upon matter, is equally unthinkable. Yet if it is the result of chance, then the world of mind and soul is only a phase of mechanics and chemistry. In that case the head of a Paul or a Homer is no greater wonder than a volcanic bomb, having essentially the same origin. If we regard it as the work of design, we are compelled to saddle all the sin and misery, all the delays and failures and wastes of the geologic ages, upon Infinite Wisdom and Goodness, together with all the famine and pestilence and carnage and miscarriages of history.

For untold millions of years the earth was given up to low, groveling, all but brainless, bestial forms, devouring and devoured; for other untold millions it was the scene of a carnival of terrible dragon-like monsters — in the sea, on the earth, and in the air — a tragedy of monstrous forms enacted upon an unstable stage that rose and sank or was overwhelmed by fire and flood. For other long ages it was the scene of ape-like creatures struggling to be man, living in caves, contending with savage beasts, hirsute, forbidding, living by tooth and claw and muscular strength more than by wit, followed by the long historical period during which man appeared and has fought his way to his present stage of development, through blood and carnage and suffering and misdirected activities, dogged by all the evil and destructive passions, obstructed and thwarted, cut off by plagues and wars, engulfed by earthquakes, devoured by fire and flood, blinded by his own ignorance, consumed by his own evil passions, yet making steady progress toward the position which he now holds in the animal kingdom.

IV. SCIENCE AND MYSTICISM

THE bogey of teleology frightens a good many honest scientific minds. To recognize anything akin to intelligence in nature, or to believe that a universal mind is immanent in, or a part of, the cosmos, is looked upon as disloyalty to the scientific spirit.

Lamarck's idea of an indwelling directing principle in organic evolution discredited him with Darwin, and with the leading biologists since his time. Yet Darwin said he could not look upon the universe as the result of chance. But he faltered before the other alternative — that any will or design lay back of it.

It is unfortunate that these words connote things purely human, and to that extent are likely to lead us astray. But are not all our terms human, even the word "astray" itself? Can we have any other? Emerson says that anything may be affirmed or denied of the Infinite, and that God can be hinted only in signs and symbols. In trying to describe time, we need a new language that differs as much from our ordinary speech as algebra differs from arithmetic. The circle and sphere are the only complete types of Infinity.

In Professor Loeb's mechanistic conception of life

there is no hint of mind or soul; all is matter and force. All the mechanists and energists and materialists unconsciously endow their matter and force with creative power, thus elevating them to the rank of a *Deus*.

Science knows no mysteries; it knows only insoluble problems and comparatively few of them. But may not one see mysteries in nature without being a mystic? Physical facts may be inexplicable, but we do not call them mysteries. The birth and development of the cell is wonderful, but can we say that it is mysterious? Does not mystery imply something occult and unknowable? Is a biologist or evolutionist to be charged with mysticism because he refuses to admit that the development of species is all a matter of chance? If he believes, for instance, that the horse as we know him was inevitable in that small beast of Eocene times, the eohippus, is he to be charged with a teleological taint? Or if we speak of the predestined course of evolution are we unfaithful to the true scientific spirit? Is not the acorn predestined to become an oak? Does growth imply a mysterious guiding force or principle? The little brown house wren that fusses and chatters here around its box on my porch has come all the way from Central America. Did something guide it? Life is full of this kind of guidance. Not much of nature can be explained by addition and subtraction; not much of it can be explained by mere mechanics, or physics; not much of it can be explained by the doctrine of chance. There are reasons behind reasons. You may give good physiological reasons why the heart beats, why the liver secretes bile, why the digestive processes go on and our food nourishes us, but can you find the mind by dissecting the brain or connect mind with matter?

Mysticism belongs to the sphere of our religious emotions, and when we read natural phenomena through these emotions we are mystical. We cannot say that the course of evolution has been directed, and we cannot say it goes by chance. The changes of the seasons are not directed; the circuit of the waters from the earth, through the sea to the clouds and back to the earth, is not directed; the orbs in their courses are not directed; the sap in the trees, the blood in our veins, are not directed; neither are these things by chance. "An inward perfecting principle" is the divinity that shapes the ends of all organisms.

Many scientific men are so shy of teleology that they tend to the other extreme and land in a world of chance.

Now, if man and all the other forms of life are the result of chance, then Chance is a very good god and should be written with a capital. No matter what we call the power out of which the universe flows, or with which it is identified, it is a veritable *Deus*.

We cannot affirm that we are the result of chance,

nor the result of design, as we use these words in our daily lives. These words apply to parts and fragments of which our lives are made up. They do not help us in dealing with the whole. We share in the life of the universe; we are a part of it, and what keeps it going keeps us going. What set evolution on foot and evolved the organic from the inorganic is the parent of us all. It is not we that are immortal; it is life, and the universe. We pass like shadows, but the sun remains — for a season. We say of a thing, or an event, that it came by chance, when we see no will like unto our own directing it; at the same time we know that the laws of matter and force control everything. Not a sparrow falls to the ground without their immutable decrees. In the same sense the hairs of our heads are numbered.

When we discuss or describe the universe in terms of experience, we are dealing in half-truths. We cannot describe a sphere in terms of angles and right lines; no more can we describe or interpret the All in terms of our own experience.

If it were Chance, or Darwin's Natural Selection, or orthogenesis, or whatever it was, that brought me and all other forms of life here, that gave me my mind and body, that put my two eyes and my two ears just where they are of most service to me, and my two arms and hands, and my two legs and feet, and all my internal organs, my double circulation, my heart to pump the blood and keep the vital machinery going, my secretions and my excretions, my lungs to lay hold of the air and purify the blood, my liver and kidneys to eliminate the poisons and effete matter, my marvelous digestive system to furnish the fuel that generates the physical power, and, more than all these things, that looked after my germ in the old Cambrian seas and brought it safely down through the hazards of the long road of evolution and developed it and made me a man, and gave me the capacity to contemplate and enjoy this amazing universe — the power or the blind force or the law of chance, I say, that could do all this is god enough for me. I want no other.

Do we expect to see the Natural Providence at work as we see man at work? Nature works from the inside. In the human sphere there is a maker and a thing made. Not so in the universe. Things are in their place without being made. Our concepts of the beginning and the end do not apply to them. The words "chance" and "design" are born of our limited knowledge.

That man or an ant or a leaf or a flower could result from the haphazard jostling together of the molecules of matter, or the units of force, is unthinkable. Could one get an intelligent sentence, or one's own name, by putting the letters of the printer's type in a hat and shaking them up till the crack of doom? — an old and trite comparison, but it seems to state the case fairly. And yet, how can a naturalist fall back upon teleology? Is not Nature sufficient unto herself? Must we inject our own little methods and makeshifts into the ways of the Eternal? We might as well try to walk off the sphere as try to compass this problem in the terms of our own experience. The inscrutable, the unthinkable, the unknowable, confront us on all sides.

So far as I can see the Creative Energy in nature has no plan nor end. Plans are the ways of the finite, not of the Infinite. Man alone has plans and ends. The Infinite cannot be defined or interpreted in terms of our human lives. It transcends all speech. To name any one thing as the purpose and end of creation is like naming the end of a sphere, or the direction of a circle. All bodies with which we deal on the earth have an upper and an under side, but the earth itself is all top side; there is no under side, though the orbs in the heavens, to our eye, have a lowest point or bottom side. Every tangible body with which we deal rests upon some other body, but the orbs float in vacuity. The irregular solid bodies with which we deal have three dimensions — length, breadth, and thickness — but, properly speaking, the sphere has none of these; it has only mass.

When we discuss or attempt to describe what we call God, or what I call the Eternal, in terms of man, as the theologians do, something within us rises up and says, No. A magnified man, or a man raised to the nth power, is not God; he is still man. I fancy that with most men the denial of a God means simply this: there is no God who can be described in the terms usually employed. One is an atheist because he cannot accept a God made in man's image. It belittles the Mystery. Our belief in God is so radical that we reject half-gods. The fatherhood of God means no more than the manhood of God, or the governorship, or the judgeship, of God.

In many respects the manlike God falls below his human prototype, being more cruel than any human being dares to be.

No, we cannot measure the Infinite Mystery with our foot-rule. Boundless space is the negation of space. We can say that there is no space in the sense that we can say that there is no God. There is no motion unless there is something at rest; there is no Infinite Good unless there is Infinite Evil. Hence we have invented a hell to balance heaven, a Devil to offset God.

The universe is a reality, though we cannot define it. Life goes on, though we cannot account for it. Boundless space exists, though words fail us in the attempt to fathom it. The earth has its center, though we do not know whether we should be standing on our heads or our heels were we to reach it. Heavenly bodies do collide, though we cannot visualize the collision. Our language fails us when we come to the ultimate questions.

ACCEPTING THE UNIVERSE

That this is the best possible world, humanly speaking, I have no doubt, yet sin and misery are on every hand. Sin and misery are terms of our own which simply express some of the conditions of our development. They are like the terms "up" and "down," "east" and "west," and "near" and "far"; they are relative. Nature knows no good and no bad; all is good; that is, all favors development. The rivers reach the sea, no matter what the obstacles in the way. The seasons come and go, no matter how delayed.

Nature's ends, so far as we can name them, are wholesale — to keep the game going, to heap the measure, to play one hand against the other. She is more solicitous about the race than about the individual. The wreck of worlds or suns in sidereal space matters little; there are infinite worlds and suns left. What would really matter would be failure of celestial mechanics. The eclipse of the sun and the moon occurring exactly on time, "without the untruth of a single second," tells how perfectly the great machine runs. The eclipse itself is an accident, but a harmless one; it is not a necessity in the movements of our system.

If man is the end of things, as we would fain believe, then why was he so long a-coming? Why will he as surely disappear from the earth? Why has he not come to other planets in our system? When he disappears from our solar system, will not the great procession go on just the same without him? No doubt of it. He is only an incident, and maybe an accident — a lucky throw of the dice.

v. IS THERE DESIGN IN NATURE?

WE cannot put to Nature the direct questions we put to ourselves. Namable purposes and designs rule our lives. Not so with the All. I told Father Goodman the other day, much to his bewilderment, that I did not think the air was made for us to breathe, nor the water for us to drink, nor food for us to eat. We breathe and drink and eat because our organization is adjusted to these things. The shoe is made over the last, not the last to fit the shoe. The organization is fitted, or fits itself, to its environment. Nature is first, man is afterwards. Is the notch in the mountain made for the road to go through? Is the land-locked harbor made to protect our shipping? Would it not be as true to say that the wind was made to fill the ship's sails, as that air was made to fill our lungs? In dealing with this question of design many persons get the cart before the horse.

Of course there is purpose or design in living things in a sense that there is not in the non-living. Every part of a living organization is purposeful. There is purpose in our lungs, our hearts, our kidneys, in short in every part of our bodies. There is purpose in the varnish on leaves, in the down and resin on buds, in the wings and hooks of seeds, in the

colors of flowers and of animals, in fact, in everything that makes for the well-being of living things.
But not in the same sense is there purpose in the
wind, the rain, the snow, the tides, the heat, the
cold, the rocks, the soil, the fountains. Animate nature struggles; inanimate nature passively submits.
Dead matter forever seeks an equilibrium; living
matter forever struggles against an equilibrium.
The waters separate the clay and the sand and the
pebbles from the soil and deposit each in its own
place; but it is not a struggle or an effort; it is mechanical adjustment. It is not an effort for certain
liquids to form crystals, or for certain elements to
combine with certain other elements and form new
compounds, but it is an effort for a tree to resist the
wind, to lift up tons of water and minerals against
gravity, to force its roots through the soil or grip
the rock, and it is an effort for the mother to bear
and nurse her young. For anything to live and grow,
effort is needful; not commonly a painful effort, but
a joyous one.

So, when we ask, Is there design in Nature? we
must make clear what part or phase of Nature we
refer to. Can we say that the cosmos as a whole
shows any design in our human sense of the word? I
think not. The Eternal has no purpose that our language can compass. There can be neither center nor
circumference to the Infinite. The distribution of
land and water on the globe cannot be the result of

design any more than can the shapes of the hills and mountains, or Saturn's rings, or Jupiter's moons. The circular forms and orbits of the universe must be the result of the laws of matter and force that prevail in celestial mechanics; this is not a final solution of the riddle, but is as near as we can come to it. One question stands on another question, and that on another, and so on, and the bottom question we can never reach and formulate. The earth rests on nothing and floats as lightly as a feather. All matter is probably only a phase of the ether, but the ether defies all proof and all negation.

How quickly we get where no step can be taken! We cannot step off the planet, though we may step off from every object on its surface. There is no heat in sunlight till it reaches the earth; heat is an experience of our bodies, and beings on the remotest planets, if there are any, may and must receive adequate heat, and beings on Mercury and Venus no more. Terrestrial physics and celestial physics must be the same, and yet celestial mechanics find no place on the surface of our planet. The laws of the cosmos bring to naught our mundane conceptions. Where are up and down, east and west, over and under, out in sidereal space? We balk at perpetual motion, yet in the heavens, and in the interior of matter, behold perpetual motion! Behold motion without friction and energy without waste or dissipation! On the earth every visible body rests on some other body, everything has a beginning and an end, but where is the beginning or the ending of the cosmos? Where, then, in this quest do we touch bottom? Nowhere. There is no bottom. Only measurable, finite things have bottoms and bounds. The immeasurable, the Infinite, is over us and under us, and our lives are like sparks against the night. But, just as we live in the heavens and do not know it, so we live and move and have our being in the Eternal. It is not afar off; it is here; we are a part of it, and as inseparable from it as from gravity.

We are not like beings who have moved into a house, made and furnished and provisioned in anticipation of our coming. We are creatures born in a house, or amid an environment to which we must slowly and more or less painfully fit ourselves. We are the consequent, not the antecedent. In a different world we should have been differently constituted. In a bigger world no doubt our bodies would have been bigger and our strength greater; with less or with more oxygen in the air, no doubt our lungs would have been different. With less light no doubt our eyes would have been larger, and with more light they would probably have been smaller. We do not feel the pressure of the atmosphere, but make the pressure more or less, and we are at once disturbed. The deep-sea fishes fairly explode when brought to the surface, and no doubt the surface fishes would be crushed in the deep sea bottoms. Just as we adjust our flying machines to the tenuity of the air, and our oversea and undersea boats to the density and weight of the water, so Nature adjusts her organisms to their environment.

Man avails himself of all possible aids. His voluntary conquests of nature are many and are constantly increasing, but his involuntary dependencies upon her are many also. He did not launch himself into this world, and he did not give his body, with all its wonderful organs and powers, the shape it has, or elect to breathe or see or hear or breed or eat or sleep. Something else determined all these things for him. What is that something else? Our fathers called it God; we call it Nature, because we live in a scientific and not in a theological age. We are pantheistic and not theistic. Our gods are everywhere, in everything created. Our minds are no longer hampered by the idea of a maker and a thing made, a ruler or a governor and a thing ruled or governed. The unity of Nature and God is a conception fostered by science. We are compelled to adjust our minds to the idea of a causeless universe, to a universe without beginning and without ending, without a maker or a designer.

Our conception of cause and effect, or beginning and ending, applies only on the surface of the earth; where currents and counter-currents, action and reaction and interaction, are in perpetual see-saw; where every body rests upon some other body, and every cause has its antecedent cause; where we can live only by dealing with parts and fragments, and by separating one thing from another. The astronomic laws and conditions, or our conceptions of them, are thrown into confusion the moment we try to apply them in our practical mundane lives. In vain we try to abolish friction and achieve perpetual motion, but the heavenly bodies move without friction, and move forever and ever. Motion is the prime condition of the universe. It is the condition or necessity we are under in this world, on the surface of this planet, that sets us on the quest of final causes and gives rise to our conceptions of the made and the maker, the good and the bad, the end and the beginning. We cannot say that we are watched over by the gods — our personification of the universal mind that pervades nature — nor that we are not watched over by them, because that were to use the language of our surface existence. All we can say is that we are a part of the cosmos, fragments of the total scheme of things, and share its laws and conditions, and that the more perfectly we adjust the nature within us to the nature without us, the better we fare. With the Infinite there is no time and no space, only an everlasting here, an everlasting now.

Yet how can puny man interpret the universe or say aught of it in terms of his mundane experiences?

VI. OUR IMPARTIAL MOTHER

THE laws and processes of Nature which to us are so beneficent, and which seem made for our especial benefit, were in full operation before life as we know it had become established. In fact, the fatherhood and motherhood of Nature are all thoughts of our own, inventions of our necessities. The paternity of gravitation and the maternity of frost and snow are in no respect different. We are the chance children — chance from our limited point of view — of an impersonal, unhuman, universal mother. We may say, humanly speaking, that Nature takes forethought of her children, but not afterthought. She provides that they shall actually appear in due time in this universe of conflicting and struggling forces, then lets them shift for themselves. They are born on the firing-line, in the field of perpetual war, and none escape unscathed. Indeed, they are moulded and adjusted and equipped by the very conditions in which the peril of their destruction lies. Gravity crushes them, and gravity gives them their powers. Fire consumes them, and water drowns them, and yet out of these things they came.

It is as if some god had planned the universe as a vast plant for the production of the myriad forms of life, each in its own place and season. In our little corner of it at a given hour of the great geologic clock one form appears, or many forms; at another hour other forms emerge, till man himself emerges as the culmination of a long line of lowly forms, many vestiges of which still cling to him. But the world is no more for man than for the mice and vermin that pester him. It is for all.

The mystery back of all — what shall we say of it? And the good and the evil that are so inextricably blended with it — what of them?

VII. BAFFLING TRUTHS

THE grand movements of Nature, both in the heavens and in the earth, are on such a scale of time and distance that without the aid of science we could get little or no hint of them. Immeasurably slow and slight they are, according to our standards. The stars are fixed points in the sky to our unaided vision. Throughout the whole historic period they have shown little or no change in their relative positions, though they are moving in varying directions at the rate of many miles a second. Come back in a thousand years and there is no change; in thirty or forty thousand years, and changes of place might be barely perceptible to an unaided eye. Not till hundreds of thousands of years would Orion, or the Big Dipper, have become noticeably distorted, and probably not till millions of years would the heavens present combinations of stars forming new constellations. The Pole Star will after millions of years probably drift far from its present position, and the

Milky Way be found in another part of the heavens. When viewed from the extreme points in space one hundred and eighty millions of miles apart which the earth's orbit around the sun gives us, the fixed stars remain fixed, they show little or no parallax. To touch but the skirts of the Infinite exhaust our powers.

The geological changes upon the surface of this earth — mere mustard-seed in space that it is — are on such a scale of time that only an unfaltering scientific faith can take them in. The mountains and the valleys seem eternal, but to the eye of the geologist they are as flitting as the summer clouds. Look upon a Catskill landscape with its long, flowing mountain-lines curving over summits three or four thousand feet high, and its deep, broad, cradle-like valleys checkered with fertile farms and homesteads, and try to think of it as all the work of the slow and gentle rains and snows — geologic time stroking them almost as gently as a mother caresses her baby. Tried by human standards we live in a stable universe; change stops with the hills and the stars; but, tried by geologic and astronomic standards, it is as unsubstantial as the snows of winter or the dews of summer. Perpetual flux and transition mark even the stars in their courses. Astronomers calculate the weight of the earth in terms of its own tons, something like six sextillion tons, but in and of itself it weighs nothing; its weight is the pull of some other body, in itself pound balances pound; it is only by detachment from it that bodies have weight. As we approach the center, a pound would be less and less; halfway down it would weigh eight ounces only; at the center weight would disappear, the pull of matter on all sides would be equal, there would no longer be up or down. Gravitation is not a demon at the center of the earth, pulling all things toward him; it is a force in every atom, pulling and being pulled in every direction. Seek the center of the pulling, and all power vanishes.

The globe is on such a scale of size with reference to our lives and powers that by no effort of the imagination can we adjust ourselves to the contradictions presented. It is not by experience, nor by living and acting, that we know it as a sphere, but by thinking and speculating. Even if we travel round it, we get no other impression than that it is an endless plain. We find no under side; it is all top side. The practical inferences we draw from looking at the moon are all contradicted by our experiences here. The lower limb of the moon is not lower, as we should find if we were to go there, and the under side of the earth is also the upper side.

Our astronomy is sound, but our actual life gives us no clue to its truths. Only when we turn philosophers do we know the tremendous voyage we are making, and then we only know it abstractly. We never can know it concretely. The swift turning of the planet under our feet, and its enormous speed in its orbit around the sun, are not revealed to our sense as motion, but as changes from night to day and from one season to another. Slow, soft, still, the moon and the sun rise and drift across the heavens, and the impassive earth seems like a ship becalmed. No hint at all of the more than rifle-bullet speed through space. It is all too big for us. The celestial machine is no machine at all to our senses, but its vast movements go on as gently and as easily as the falling of the dew or the blooming of the flowers, and almost as unconsciously to us as the circulation of the blood in our hearts.

We are in the heavens and are a part of the great astronomical whirl and procession, and know it not. It is symbolical of our lives generally. We do not realize that we are a part of Nature till we begin to think about it. Our lives proceed as if we were two — man and Nature — two great antagonistic or contrary facts, but the two are one; there is only Nature. We can draw circle within circle, and circle around circle, but we cannot circumscribe Nature. That is the fact over all.

As struggling human beings we diverge from one another, oppose one another, defeat one another. All our differences and antagonisms arise from our need of action and of living. The lesson of the sphere is hard to learn, hard to state. Our powers of detachment are hardly equal to it. Our lives are rounded by the great astronomic curves. The contradictions which the intellect reveals, the unthinkable mysteries that surround us, the heavens over us, the earth under us always — the relativity of all things — thus does thought set us adrift on a shoreless sea.

VIII. SENSE CONTRADICTIONS

BERGSON says that we are in trouble the moment we think of a creator and a thing created; in other words, the moment we apply to the universe as a whole the concepts which our practical lives yield us. The only alternative I see is to think of the universe as uncreated, which, I confess, does not make the problem much easier. I try to help myself out by saying that our concepts are formed in a world in which we deal with parts and fragments, lines and angles on the surface of a sphere, and not with the sphere as a whole. Our senses do not reveal the earth to us as a globe, but as a boundless plain with no under side; we find no limits, and if we continue our search long enough, we come back to the place from which we set out, but from the opposite direction.

When we try to think in terms of spheres and solar systems, our everyday concepts avail us very little; in fact, they set us down wrong-end up. We look at the moon or the sun and we say, Surely if we were at the South Pole of either of these bodies, we should be as truly on the under side of it as the fly is when it alights at the South Pole of the globe in our study. We should be in a position opposite to that which we should occupy at the North Pole. That every point on the surface of a cosmic sphere should be on top, or rather that there should be no top, and no bottom; that these concepts should be abolished; that if two inhabited globes should come in collision, each would seem to the people upon the other to be falling down out of the heavens upon them; that out in sidereal space not even the Huns could drop bombs, or send up balloons, because there would be no up and no down — when we grasp these facts, I say, we are at the end of our tether; we not only do not know "where we are at," but we find there is no "at." Our minds can deal with the cosmos only in an abstract or mathematical way. As a concrete fact even our little earth is too much for us. Not merely too big, it contradicts all our experience. If we could build a sphere a mile through, or ten miles or a hundred miles, or ten thousand miles through, could we stand upon it at the South Pole? When we think of the daily revolutions of the earth upon its axis, we are compelled to think of it as turning over, because it brings the sun above us by day and beneath us by night, and hence the puzzle to the unlettered mind as to why the lakes and ponds do not all spill out.

Among the heavenly bodies other laws prevail; there is motion without friction or dissipation of energy; there is no body at rest; there is no motion in right lines, but only in curved lines; there is no beginning nor ending; there is only eternal progression; and this is a condition of things that throws our mental adjustments all out of gear. The problem of God, the problem of creation, the problem of future life, throw our mental adjustments out of gear in the same way.

There is order and harmony in our own solar system and doubtless in countless others in the immensity of space, but the cosmos as a whole does not seem to present this harmony, as collisions actually occur. Astronomers tell us that the units of the starry hosts are moving in all directions and that collisions are inevitable, though at such vast intervals, owing to the inconceivable spaces, that human time can take no note of them. A billion of our years, like a billion of our miles, count for but little in the infinitudes of the universe.

When we try to think that the universe had a creator, that there was a time when it did not exist, that it was called into being by a power apart from itself, do we not fall down completely? We can, of course, think in arbitrary terms; our imaginations are equal to almost any feat (Lewis Carroll's was equal to "Alice in Wonderland"; Dante's was equal to making the world shudder over his pictures of the inferno): but the understanding has to have solid ground to go upon, and where is the solid ground in our idea of creation? We are off the sphere, alone in space, face to face with the Infinite, and we have no language in which to express ourselves.)

IX. MAN A PART OF NATURE

WE habitually think or speak of ourselves as something apart from Nature, as belonging to some higher order of reality, when, in fact, we are as much a part of the total scheme of things as are the trees and the beasts of the field. True, we are separated from them by a gulf, but the gulf has been bridged, and bridged by Nature, and both sides are equally her territory.

Nature is the one supreme reality, the sum total of the visible and invisible bodies and forces that surround us, out of which we came and of which we form a part. Nature is all things to all men, because she is the larger fact, and holds an infinite diversity in an all-embracing unity.

When we come to look upon man in this light, when we see his whole civilization and all his achievements upon the earth — his science, his philosophy, his art, his religion, yea, his follies and crimes and superstitions, his wars and hatreds, as well as his heroism and devotion — as parts of Nature, as expressions of the same total cosmic energy as are all things else, we have gained an astronomic point of view; we see things in orbic completeness.

Nature is all-inclusive. We cannot draw a circle around that circle. We have so long been wont to solve our riddles by invoking the supernatural that the habit has become ingrained. We can only do as Carlyle did, feed our minds with words and fall back upon the natural-supernatural.

Our attitudes toward Nature differ as widely as do our occupations, our characters, and our temperaments. There is the direct, practical attitude of the farmer, the miner, the engineer, the sailor, the sportsman, the traveler, and the explorer; there is the gay and holiday attitude of the camper-out and the picnicker; there is the sympathetic and appreciative attitude of the nature-lover; there is the imaginative and creative attitude of the artist and the poet; there is the more or less rapt and mystical attitude of the religious enthusiast; there is the inquisitive and experimental attitude of the man of science; and there is the meditative and speculative attitude of the philosopher.

We almost invariably personify Nature and read our own traits and limitations into her. We say she is wise or she is foolish; she is cruel or she is kind; she fails or she succeeds. The early philosophers said that Nature abhorred a vacuum. Darwin says that she "tells us in the most emphatic manner that she abhors perpetual self-fertilization." There are times when the most rigid man of science humanizes Nature in this way. We look upon ourselves as taking liberties with her; we discipline her and train her in the ways she should go for our good; we pit her forces against one another. Her flowers, her birds, her sunsets, her rainbows, her waterfalls, her mountain lakes, her ocean-shores, her midnight skies, at times move us and lift us above ourselves. On the other hand, there are times when we frown upon her, or despitefully use her and call her hard names. When her storms or her frosts or her blights or her droughts or her insect hordes destroy our crops, or lay waste our forests or sweep away our buildings or kill our cattle or inundate our towns and villages, we instinctively look upon her as our enemy, and, so far as we are able, arm ourselves against her. Emerson speaks of Nature as that "terrific or beneficent force." It is both. Indeed, we may use a stronger adjective and say that at times it is a malevolent force.

We ascribe all our human qualities and traits to Nature. Indeed, we can hardly speak of her without personifying her. As we are a part of her, how can we fail to see our own traits in her? At least, how else can we interpret her except in terms of our own being? Early man did this entirely. All the natural forces and appearances took on his own image, and were for or against him. When we seek to interpret Nature we still do it in the terms of literature, of poetry. We humanize her, which means, of course, that we interpret ourselves. Nature reflects the spirit we bring to her. She is gay, somber, beautiful, winsome, repellent, wise or foolish, just in the degree in which we ourselves are capable of these emotions or possess these qualities. She is terrifying because we have a capacity for terror. She is soothing when we are in a mood to be soothed. She is sublime only so far as we have the capacity to experience this emotion.

It is our reactions to Nature that give rise to the qualities we ascribe to her. The music of the æolian harp is not in the wind; its origin is the reaction of the harp to the wind, but it is not music until it reaches the human ear. The colors of the landscape are not in the rocks and trees and waters, but in the experiences of the eye when the vibrations of ether which we call light are reflected back to it from these objects.

We create the world in which we live. I love Nature, but Nature does not love me. Love is an emotion which rocks and clouds do not feel. Nature loves me in my fellow beings. The breezes caress me, the morning refreshes me, the rain on the roof soothes me — that is, when I am in a mood to be caressed and refreshed and soothed. The main matter is the part I play in these things. All is directed to me and you because we are adjusted to all. No more is the kite or the sail adjusted to the wind, the water-wheel to the falling water, than are we adjusted to outward Nature. She is the primary and everlasting fact; we, as living beings, are the secondary and temporary facts.

X. THE FITTEST TO SURVIVE

THE survival of the fittest does not mean the survival of the best from the human point of view. The lower orders of humanity are better fitted to survive than the higher orders—hardier, more prolific, having a fuller measure of life. The cultivated plants — wheat, corn, rye, barley, oats — are less fitted to survive than what we call weeds. The latter can shift for themselves, but the former cannot.

We lament the decay of the native Anglo-Saxon stock in this country, and the increase of the races from southern Europe and from the Orient. They stand our pitiless sunlight better than do the descendants of our Puritan ancestors. From our point of view this rule of natural selection will not result in a superior race, but in an inferior; not in better men, but in better animals. Character and intellect win in those fields where character and intellect tell, but where muscle and brawn and vitality tell more they fail.

The Japanese have great power of survival; they are hardy, prolific, and pushing. The Germans also have great survival power, greater than the French; they are more prolific, more materialistic, nearer the brutes; they are not handicapped with much soul. They are morally blind, but intellectually clever. Their moral blindness and insensibility have resulted in their downfall. Great Britain leads the

European nations because she is not only hardy and prolific, but she also has the gift of empire; she builds upon law and order; she establishes justice and fair play.

In the Darwinian sense the Jews are the fittest to survive of all the races of man. They are prolific and grasping; they will always get what belongs to them, and a little more; they are bound to possess the earth. The only drawback I see is that they do not take kindly to the soil. Trade alone will not give a nation the supremacy.

XI. THE POWER OF CHOICE

THINK how we come into the world, what an important thing it is to each of us and to the world, and yet how fortuitous and haphazard it all is, and what precautions are often taken to prevent our coming!

See the deformed, the half-witted, the low-browed, the degenerate, that come. The great army of the common, the few capable of higher and finer things. Nature apparently finds her account in one class the same as in the other, in Pat as well as in Paul, in the inferior races as well as in the higher.

In our manufacturing affairs we aim to turn out the best article possible — the best shoe, the best hat, the best gun, the best book; but Nature makes no such effort in the case of man, though she does in the case of the lower orders. Probably every individual bird or bug or four-footed beast in a state of nature is perfect of its kind, that is, suited to its place in the scheme of organic life. But how different with man! It is the price he pays for his freedom, his power of choice. The birds and the beasts have no power of choice, they are entirely in the hands of Nature. They are all moulded to one pattern.

The advantage that comes to man from his power of choice is greater variation, hence greater progress. He crosses or reverses or turns aside the laws of Nature, or bends them to his will, and for this privilege he pays the price of idiocy, deformity, and the vast mass of commonplace humanity. His gain is now and then men of exceptional ability, geniuses, who lead the race forward. We know that every improved breed of chicken or sheep or swine will come true, but we do not know in anything like the same degree of certainty that the Emersons and the Lincolns and the Tennysons will repeat and continue the type. Cultivated fruit relapses in the seed, and cultivated persons often do the same.

On the other hand, rude and ordinary humanity now and then far transcends itself in its offspring, just as the new and choice apple or peach or plum has its humble origin in a seedling.

XII. ILLUSIONS

In his "Conduct of Life" Emerson has an essay on "Illusions" in which he describes the semblance to

midnight skies paved with stars which the guide
produces in the Mammoth Cave by hiding himself
and throwing the rays of his torch athwart the ceil-
ing set thick with transparent rock crystals. The
effect is quite startling. For the moment it is hard to
resist the conviction that you are actually looking
upon the cloudless sky at night. But in reality is not
the noonday sky just as much of an illusion, except
that there are no mimic stars? The blue dome overhead is an illusion. There is no dome there. The
sky is a mere apparition. It is not a body or a
reality as it seems to be; it is mere empty space,
though it has the effect upon us of a vast blue dome.
How genial and inviting it looks when we see it
peeping through the clouds, and how glorious when
we see it swept free from clouds! Its purity, its
serenity, its elevated character, move us to regard
it as the abode of superior beings. The telescope
dispels our illusions; the sky is not a transparent
realm, but only an extension of earthly conditions.
Heaven, the abode of the blest, takes its name from
this negation of vacancy. Our notions of a personal
God are similar illusions. God is as real as the sky
is, and no more so, even though in our devout
moods we lift our eyes heavenward and identify him
with this comforting illusion.

All our life illusions brood over us. The night
is only a shadow — the negation of light; and
yet it plays a part in our lives as real as that of

health or friends or climate, as real, but of another kind.

Time itself is an illusion. The future does not exist nor the past; yet how are our lives influenced by the memory of the one and our anticipations of the other!

The world is, indeed, full of illusion. We fancy that luminous bodies shoot out rays of light such as we appear to see when we look at them. We see beams and scintillations when we look at the stars and the sun; but is it not all a trick of the eye? The light from a luminous body goes out in all directions, not in separated rays, but as vibrations in the ether. When we throw a stone into a still pool of water a wave motion is set up which spreads in concentric circles. But the vibrations called "light," considered as a whole, assume the form of a sphere; they go from the luminous body to every point of a hollow sphere. We see a star as a bright point in the sky, but if the universe were full of eyes, every eye could see that star; its light goes to every point of the hollow sphere of Infinity. But no more than does the light of the candle in your hand, or the lamp on your table go to Infinity, if unobstructed. Stars which cannot be seen by the most powerful telescope must yet radiate their light into infinite space. Is that light lost? Modern science seems to hold to the view that in the ether of space no rays of light can ever be lost. What becomes of them? It is certain that a wavelet in a lake can be lost if the lake is large enough. It soon dies out. It becomes dissipated. Energy cannot be destroyed, but it can be scattered or turned into heat or light or electricity, and the waves that break and die upon the beach, no matter how cold they are, give up their energy as heat. They must raise the temperature some fraction of a degree.

XIII. IS NATURE SUICIDAL?

EMERSON never committed himself to a belief in immortality as usually understood — continued existence in another world; but he was always on the lookout for hints and suggestions to spur his lagging faith on the subject. He read Martial and praised his literary faculty. He is the true writer, he said, a chemical and not a mechanical mixture: "Martial suggests again, as every purely literary book does, the immortality. We see we are wiser than we were: we are older. Can Nature afford to lose such improvements? Is Nature a suicide?" The same questions I have heard Whitman ask, questions asked probably by thoughtful men in all ages.

But are not such questions prompted by our own petty economies? We must save what we have gained. Not so Nature. Gain and loss with her are one. All is hers. She has infinite time, and infinite abundance. How can she afford so many dead worlds and burnt-out suns scattered throughout sidereal

space, like boulders in a New England field? How
can she afford to wait millions of years before life
comes to the superior planets, if it ever comes?
What economy is that which strews the way of evolution with untold numbers of extinct species?
What economy is that which makes one species
prey upon another? — which undoes with one hand
what she achieves with the other? Nature was millions of years in bringing man out of the earth, —
the end and flower of her whole scheme from our
point of view, — and probably in far less time he
will have disappeared from the earth. How can
she afford it? "Is Nature suicidal?" She certainly
is, tried by our standards. Not that she is less than
we, but so inconceivably more. She plays the game
for her own amusement. She evaporates the rivers
and the seas, confident that the water will come back
again. She keeps the currents going; the ebb and
flow never cease. Night and day, life and death, go
hand in hand. Her "improvements" are improvements for a day, an hour, a moment — like snow-
flakes on the river — "a moment white, then gone
forever." They are crystals that perish, flowers that
fall. Nature knows no exhaustion; she can repeat
the process continuously. Only the unlimited is inexhaustible. The infinite goes on forever. Our economics pale in the face of Nature's prodigalities. A
race like the Greeks perishes, and Nature's treasury
is still full. Every spring in our climate the marvel

of leaf and flower is repeated in the plants and forests, and every fall the work is undone. The great, the noble, the heroic, youth, age, manhood, womanhood, fail and disappear, and still the game goes on. The rivers drain the hills and mountains, and still they never run dry. Spring and summer do not exhaust the fertility of Nature. The rivers carry the soil into the sea, but they do not carry it off the globe. We cannot defertilize the earth. What the seas lose, the clouds gain; what the clouds lose, the earth gains; what the hills lose, the sea gains; and so the circle is complete.

Nature has her own economies that answer to our own. In the use of means to an end, as in the living world, there must be economy of time, of space, of power; there must be adjustments, compensations, and so on. In the tropics vegetation takes its time. No hurry; the heat does not fail. In the temperate zone there is less time, and the pace of vegetation is faster. In the frigid zone it is faster still, the time is brief; there is no prodigality of leaf and stalk and flower; hurry up is the cry. The stalk is short, the flowering is brief, the goal is the seed which must be matured. In our climate, if a plant gets a later start, or is cut down and compelled to bloom again, — for example, the burdock, — how it hastens, how it pushes out its seed-vessels from the main stalk! The late fall dandelions do not indulge in long stalks; they bloom close to the ground and develop their down-seed balloons or parachutes at once. In the Far North the willow and birch are mere running vines, but they achieve fruit.

The economy of living nature is the basis of our economy; we improve upon it, we take a short cut, we save time and save power. We trim our trees, we remove obstructions, we fertilize, we graft, we sow and plant. Nature is prodigal of her spawn and pollen to offset the element of chance that enters into the action of the winds and the waves.

The wild creatures have their instinctive economies and ways of getting on in the world. They prepare for the winter; they provide for their young; they practice the arts of concealment; they are wise for their own good; they do not commit suicide. The plants have their economies, and the insects have theirs, but when we talk of the economy of Nature, we are beyond soundings. Nature cannot spend more than she earns; her ledgers always balance; her capital cannot be impaired. There is no waste, in our sense, in the universe. Can you destroy magnetism by pulverizing the magnet? Would electricity be quenched if no storm-cloud ever again appeared in the sky?

XIV. THE PERSISTENCE OF ENERGY

Is it not reassuring to know that we cannot get out of the universe — that whatever is real about us cannot be destroyed, but can only suffer change?

All the elements that enter into my body must persist; they always have persisted through all the vicissitudes of astronomic and geologic time. We are as sure of that as we are sure of anything, and we are sure that they will continue in some form to exist. We believe it without proof. Our scientific faith carries us over this gulf — our faith in the oneness and integrity of the universe. Is there anything real, in the same sense, in what we call our minds or souls? Huxley was convinced that consciousness was as real as matter and energy, and must persist like them — persist in other persons who follow us; but how about our individual selves? And how about consciousness when the race of man becomes extinct? We can only take refuge in the thought that consciousness will dawn and continue in other worlds through all time, or rather endless time, since the all of a thing implies limits. Equally to make consciousness coeval with matter and energy, we must think of it as having existed in other worlds throughout an endless and beginningless past. But my consciousness and your consciousness are bound up with certain combinations of matter which we know are unstable — in fact, are the result, in a sense, of their instability, their ceaseless change.

In the final change, which we call death, what happens to consciousness? When we try to think of it in terms of our actual experience with tangible bodies, we think of it as gone out, non-existent, as truly so as is the flame of the candle when we blow it out, or as is the star form of the snowflake when it is melted. Does it help us any to think of the soul, or consciousness, in terms of the imponderable bodies — light, electricity, radio-activity? Do all these wireless messages that go forth into the air, go on forever? Do these impulses reach the farthest stars, and still persist? Do our thoughts persist upon the ether? Here, in this room, here in this air that you may inclose with your two hands, are vibrating wireless messages from far and near, though we are not able to detect them. Here also the ether may be tremulous with the thoughts of our friends on the other side of the globe, yes, and with the thoughts of our friends who have ceased to live, as we know life. The ether of space may still be vibrating with the thoughts of Plato and Aristotle, of Moses and Solomon.

Do we impress ourselves momentarily upon the ether around us, and is this what the mediums and the clairvoyants recover? Is the persistence of our thoughts upon the ether the secret of the mind-reader's art, and of all the marvelous things disclosed by psychic research? Is this the only immortality, the immortality of the endless persistence of vibrations from our brains? Or must we think of our personalities as disembodied and drifting about as separate entities in the great Nowhere?

Though a dreamer and an idealist, I am only truly interested in a natural explanation of things — an explanation that is in harmony with our experiences in this world. The so-called supernatural explanation does not interest me at all. We cannot grasp it and bring it to the test of reason and experience. It is like a bridge with one or more spans missing — only faith can carry us over, and faith that has nothing to stand upon cannot really carry us over. It travels in a circle, and leaves us where it found us.

Energy is certainly one of the realities of the cosmos, though we may not be able to form a concept of it as we do of matter. We cannot visualize it. We know it only through its effects upon tangible bodies. Why may there not be a principle of life or vitality as real as is energy — another form of energy which we can know only through its effects upon matter; inseparably bound up with matter as energy is; not with all matter, but with a limited amount of matter, as is magnetism — a peculiar form of force or energy, dependent for its manifestations upon well-defined conditions and reaching its highest manifestations in the mind or consciousness of man. Spirit, as we name it, is only a word which stands for no verifiable reality — something separable from matter and independent of it. What victims we are of words! When we get a name for a thing we are persuaded the thing exists. The vital process is inseparable from the physical processes; it supplements or controls them, but is more than they are. Life is not a spirit, but a form of energy potential in matter, and developed and active when the conditions are right. A living body is moved by a new force just as truly as a piece of magnetized steel is moved by a new force, or as truly as a new force streams through the telegraph-wires — a transformation of other forces, and behaving in a new way, and producing new results. There is nothing new under the sun; all are made of one stuff; but there are endless transformations and permutations of this one stuff, and one of them is the phenomenon of life, or vitality.

Electricity is not matter, but it is the most unmistakable and ubiquitous form of energy known to us. The human mind is a phenomenon of matter; how related to the electro-magnetic world we know not, but undoubtedly in some way bound up with it.

To discuss the soul or attempt to interpret it in terms of these mundane forces will, of course, offend the so-called spiritualists. So long have we been taught to look upon the soul as belonging to another world, another order of things from that of the body. Whitman says that soul and body are one, and leaves his puzzled reader to solve the riddle as best he can. Heaven and earth are one in the same sense — there is nothing alien or irreconcilable between them. The flower and its stalk, the perfume and the root, are one in the same sense. The mind resides in the gray matter of the brain, and depends upon the food we eat as truly as does the body.

When we discuss these questions in terms of our religious training we reach far different conclusions, or, rather, we start with far different conclusions; but how can we relate these conclusions to the concrete facts as we know them?

There is enough that is verifiable in clairvoyance and mind-reading and mental healing to convince us that we are immersed in a world of subtle forces that ordinarily we wot not of; that in some way a process of give and take between us and these things is constantly going on, and that our relation to them is at least one form or suggestion of our immortality. We are a part of the wave of energy that sweeps through the cosmos, as truly as the drops of the sea hold and convey the tidal impulse. We know, or think we know, the sources of this tidal impulse, but the attraction between earth and moon and sun is reciprocal — a give-and-take process — and is only a phase of the sum total (if the Infinite can be said to have a sum total) of the energy of the cosmos.

The magnet and magnetism are one. If you melt or pulverize the magnet, you dissipate, but do not destroy the magnetism. The clouds come and go; now we see them, and then there is only blue sky where they were. Change, but not destruction. When the thunder-cloud disperses, where are its terrible bolts? Withdrawn, probably, or redistributed into the inmost recesses of matter or of the ether. The energy of the human brain and body cannot be destroyed by death, only changed. If consciousness is a force, then it, too, must persist. It seems, in some way, the equivalent of the force of the body, at least one of its phenomena. But is it anything more than the analogue of the light which the electric spark emits, and which is light only to the eye? Consciousness is such only to itself; it cannot be seen or felt or known by other consciousnesses. What we know about the consciousnesses of others, we know through our own.

In the presence of the death of our friends no doubt this is a cheerless and depressing kind of philosophy, but in the pursuit of truth, if we are sincere, we do not seek to administer to, or to warm and cheer our human affections. Our seriousness will be measured by the extent to which we put all these things behind us. Heroic self-denial finds a field here as well as in the struggles of life. We do not want to cheer ourselves with illusions, no matter how welcome they are. "All's right with the world." The laws of life and death are as they should be. The laws of matter and force are as they should be; and if death ends my consciousness, still is death good. I have had life on those terms, and somewhere, somehow, the course of nature is justified. I shall not be imprisoned in that grave where you are to bury my body. I shall be diffused in great Nature, in the soil, in the air, in the sunshine, in the hearts of those who love me, in all the living and flowing currents of the world, though I may never again in my entirety be embodied in a single human being. My elements and my forces go back into the original sources out of which they came, and these sources are perennial in this vast, wonderful, divine cosmos.

XIV

SOUNDINGS

I. THE GREAT MYSTERY

NO man in his senses can fail to grant the reality of the Great Mystery, the inscrutable and unspeakable Something which lies back of us and works in and through us, the vast Cosmic Energy of which we and all forms of life are manifestations, and in which we live and move and have our being, call it physical energy or psychic power, or what you will.

We are not here by our wills; we do not have our eyes and ears, and the other wonderful mechanisms of our bodies, and all our varied instincts and capacities and aspirations of our own will and invention. We have little or nothing to do with the functioning of our various bodily organs, scarcely more than we have to do with the color of our eyes, our innate dispositions, and our mental aptitudes. In something not of us, at least not subject to our wills and wishes, is to be sought the explanation of our appearance, and that of all other forms of life, in this world. In other words, we are an integral part of a system of things which transcends our powers and baffles our understanding. After we have granted all this, can we still feel the solid ground beneath our feet in accepting the explanation and interpretation which any of the formal religious systems, old or new, place upon it? I think not.

In the presence of the midnight skies, of the creative and destructive cosmic processes constantly going on in the awful depths of the sidereal space, of suns and systems coming in and going out like blooming and fading flowers, in the presence of the geological and biological histories of the globe, or of the histories of the different nations and races of the globe, does not most of our Christian mythology seem utterly childish?

How strange that we should crave a creed or a belief that goes outside of our experimental knowledge; that is independent of it, not subject to its tests and limitations; something afar off and irrational and inexplicable, and beyond the reach of time and change! Who is the philosopher who said that we are guided by our common sense in everything but our religious beliefs?

We can taste and see and touch and smell and eat and drink and measure and accumulate and organize and assimilate scientific knowledge; it gives us a place whereon to stand our Archimedean lever with which we can move the world and the whole sidereal system of worlds. But with our so-called theological knowledge, and with much of our metaphysical knowledge, it is like trying to move with a lever the mountain upon which one stands.

Furthermore, grant that the religious sense of mankind is real, one of the most real things in life,— so real and valuable that the life, the literature, and the art which have it not seem shallow and ephemeral, — a living sense of the Infinite Mystery in which we are embosomed and our constant relation to it, — grant this, I say, and yet our creeds and systems of salvation do not minister to it. They are too legal; they know and explain too much. With them the administration of the universe is as simple and judicial as a police court, save that in human courts of justice there is no deputed sin or atonement. This is a gratuitous, manufactured mystery of the theologians, as are the Trinity and the saving grace of rites and ceremonies.

Science has real mysteries. Catalysis is one. How or why the presence of one body should cause two other bodies to unite chemically without parting with an atom of their own substance — as in several cases in industrial chemistry — is certainly a mystery. On the strength of such and similar facts in chemistry, shall we image or invent a whole category of mysteries which are beyond the reach of verification?

What mystery hovers about all chemical reactions! What a miracle that two invisible gases, such as oxygen and hydrogen, should, when chemically united, produce a body so utterly unlike either as is water! The turning of water into wine is as nothing in comparison, but even that feat we want to see done if we are to believe it.

What a mystery shrouds the whole subject of electricity and electro-magnetism! A sort of disembodied force, working its will upon matter and yet subject to none of the laws of matter. Spirit? — but a spirit we can evoke at will, and make to do our bidding, to run our errands, a spirit more friendly than unfriendly. How prone the common mind is to think that because a thing is mysterious it must be true!

As I have already emphasized, as man is a part of Nature, so are all his creeds and myths, his religions and his philosophies, a part of Nature. What validity does that give them? What support is lent to our creed by the fact that it has been slowly evolved out of the religious experiences of the centuries? Our sense of truth is also an evolution, and varies from age to age. That a thing is a part of Nature does not settle its value. Shadows are a part of Nature; puffballs, fungi, marsh-gas, disease-germs, and a thousand other undesirable things are a part of Nature.

Although the various religious systems of mankind must have their natural history, I regard them only as so many diverse attempts to clothe the spirit against the cosmic chill of the vast, unhoused, unsanctified, immeasurable out-of-doors of the universe. This they do in varying degrees, and will con-

tinue to do, some appealing to one type of mind, or
— shall we say? — one stage of development, some
to another. The philosopher looks on and smiles, or
pities, and is content.

II. THE NATURAL ORDER

Even great thinkers like Mr. Balfour recoil from
naturalism and cheerfully embrace supernaturalism.
Mr. Balfour finds the key to the fundamental problems of life in the miracle of the Incarnation. He in-
jects into the natural order a theological concept,
and the riddle of man's life is solved. To the naturalist such a conclusion is as impossible as to hope to
quench his thirst with the symbols, H_2O.

We may say every man born of woman is an incarnation of the Infinite spirit, and the hyperbole
may stand, but to affirm that one particular man in
the historic period was an incarnation in an entirely other and more significant sense, is to read
magic into matters of common sense. It is an imaginary solution. It is an appeal from the natural to
the non-natural. It is offering an artificial solution
to a natural problem. One might as well attribute a
failure of the crops to one of the political parties, or
an epidemic of disease to an historical document.
The doctrine of the Incarnation is as far outside the
realm of natural law as is magic, and to see in this
the master key to creation is like ascribing all the
sin and misery of the world to Adam's transgression

in the Garden of Eden. The childish plan of salvation of our fathers is as good as any other so long as
it holds men up to higher standards of life and of
thought; but the day is fast passing when it can do
this; natural standards must in the end as surely
prevail in religion as in our daily lives.

The nature that we see about us is enough for all
forms of life except man; why should he flatter himself that his appearance and life demand something
extra, some miracle, something mysterious and incomprehensible? Why not invest the gods we have
and know with the extra power demanded, rather
than appeal to gods we know not? How the fire
warms us, how our food nourishes us, how we sprang
from a microscopic germ and grew to be the men we
are, are miracles enough. Every living thing is a
miracle as wonderful as the Immaculate Conception
or the Incarnation, but of a different order. If I
knew how the meat and bread which the poet eats is
turned into poetry, or how the pond-lily weaves its
satin and gold out of the muck and slime of the
creek-bottom, I should possess a secret that would
make me cease to wonder at the so-called "miracles." In the face of the marvels we hourly see about
us in living Nature, why should we look afar off and
invent marvels of a new order? Why should we invent impossible problems, and then invent impossible explanations of them?

The nature gods we know; we live in daily and

hourly converse with them; we see and know that we are dependent upon them every moment of our lives. These gods — air, water, fire, earth — and the greater gods whose eyes blink to us in the midnight skies, why not credit them with the gifts that we ascribe to the imaginary gods of the supernatural?

The more we search into the ways of Nature, the more wonderful and potent we find them to be. It may be that if we could penetrate to the true inwardness of matter, we should find the key to the mystery of the soul and the master key to all our problems. But we feel that we must look afar off, we must have recourse to the strange and the miraculous. How the impossible does attract us! Even the fantastic may be made the basis of a religious cult. In Florida, in a remote, secluded place we found a religious sect, embracing men and women of culture and refinement, who upheld the social and civic virtues and cultivated the industrial arts, yet who deemed it essential for their soul's salvation to disbelieve all our popular astronomy, and hold to the idea that, instead of living on the outside of a globe, we live inside of a hollow sphere, and that the sun, moon, and stars are appendages of this sphere, and not at all what we ordinarily take them to be. The expounders of this faith are not at all disturbed by such facts as a ship at sea dropping below the horizon, or an eclipse of the moon showing the shadow of a round body falling upon it. Such appearances only confirm their theory. These Florida fanatics defy common sense and the exact demonstrations of science. Our supernaturalists superinduce another order above and around the order we call "natural," and in a theological concept, the Incarnation, link the two together. That they are linked at any other point is not claimed. In the age of miracles they were linked at many points and on many occasions. Any saint could link them together at will, and reverse or hold up the processes of the natural order and substitute those of the supernatural.

Such events as miracles come very easy to the mind imbued with the old theological concepts. Why should not this omnipotent being who made and rules the world and all that it holds, and who has a scheme of his own to carry out with regard to man, step in at any time and annul natural law or link it up with the supernatural? Belief in the theory of such a being cuts many knots, while it ties others that defy all our wits.

Life is so great a mystery that we need not invent others. We have the proof of life always, what proof have we of the Incarnation? We know what destroys life, what favors it, what conserves it, but we do not know its origin. We know something about the stars, and we know the constellations are only imaginary groupings. The historical events upon which our creeds are founded are of the same character. The Trinity is a constellation. The miraculous birth of Christ is a constellation. The fixed stars of man's moral nature and religious aspirations are alone real. All the mythologies built upon them are as fanciful as Orion and the Big Dipper. All the various religions of the world, with all their supernatural features, are a part of the natural history of man's religious instincts. Man's craving for the supernatural is as natural as our discounting of the present moment, and no more significant. The natural becomes trite and commonplace to us and we take refuge in an imaginary world above and beyond it. The understanding becomes sated, and we long for something we cannot understand.

III. LOGIC AND RELIGIOUS BELIEFS

Of late years I am often moved to say to myself: "Why kick the old theology after it is dead?" — as I have often been tempted to do. It is almost like spurning the bodies of one's father and mother. The old creeds may be outworn, but they have fathered and mothered us all. They have served and saved untold generations of men. Christianity, mythical and irrational as much of it is, has yet been the salvation of the world for nineteen centuries. Of course it has been a source of evil as well as of good, as all religions are, but the good has greatly predominated. In fact, it is the bed-rock upon which our civilization is founded. It has saved men in this world by inspiring them with the desire to be worthy of a better and future world.

We are saved, I often say, not so much by the truth of what we believe, as by the truth of our belief, by its genuineness, its power over our imaginations, its hold upon our character, its fostering of an incentive to right conduct and noble deeds. Whether it be Catholicism or Calvinism or Methodism or Quakerism or Christian Science or the Japanese ancestor worship or Buddhism, if it holds us to higher ideals and gives sobriety and sincerity to our lives, that is its true function.

In fact, any religion is good which supplies a man or a people with a workable theory of the universe. In practical matters, in dealing with real facts and forces, man is compelled to be logical or he comes to grief — he must keep fire and powder apart. But in his religion and speculations he is bound by no such necessity; he is free to indulge the wildest dreams.

Man does not expect fire or flood or frost or wind or rain to favor him. He does not put fluids in leaky vessels, nor a leaky roof over his head, nor plant his house on a foundation of sand. His carpenter's level does not lie, nor his plumb-line make a mistake. But in his religion he may be as capricious and fantastic as he pleases; he has a free hand; he may even flog his gods if they displease him, and it is all the same.

His creed is a passport to an entirely different world.

The religious sect which I visited in Florida, which held that we live upon the inside of a hollow sphere, treated our astronomy with scorn, yet seemed to live sober, sane lives, and to do honest work. But if they carried out the theory of the hollow sphere in practice, in their navigation, in their clocks and sun-dials, or in anything else, how quickly they would come to grief!

Christianity is a workable hypothesis; it solves the problem of life to vast numbers of persons; but how irrational and puerile its philosophy, founded upon the myth of the fall of Adam in the Garden of Eden! Destroy this myth and you have cut off the tap-root of Christianity. But do we not know, in the light of evolution, that man's course has been upward and not downward, that his "fall" was, in fact, development into a higher state of being?

Thinking men must find some sort of a solution of the problems of the universe, and feeling men and women must have some tangible, concrete thing that in a measure satisfies their emotional natures. The human heart cannot live on cold philosophical abstractions. The ceremonies and observances and rituals of the Church give one something he can see and feel. For my own part I do not need this sort of thing. Every day is a Sabbath day to me. All pure water is holy water, and this earth is a celestial abode. It has not entered into the mind of any man to see and feel the wonders and the mysteries and the heavenly character of this world.

All religions look away from the earth to some fairer and better abode, quite oblivious of the fact that heaven, wherever we find it, will be of our own making. If we do not find it here, we shall not find it anywhere. But the great mass of struggling, toiling, human kind must be comforted and encouraged by the prospect of emancipation from the grossness and suffering of this world. Goethe acutely said to let those who could not have literature or art or science, have religion.

Think of the many sturdy, God-fearing, churchgoing, simple folk one has known in his youth — how impossible their creeds, but how worthy their lives! It requires the heroic fiber to accept the creed of Calvinism; it is a proposition that tries a man's mettle. The current generation is too frivolous and empty to be impressed by it; not one in a thousand is man enough to accept it. The movies suit them better. But what granite stuff went to the making of our Pilgrim fathers!

Cease all Christian effort, all organized Christian charities, all Christian enterprises in the fields of education, social betterment, sanitation, amelioration of the masses, and our civilization would suffer. Then why rail at the old creeds, I say again. They prepared the way for science, and for the religion of nature. Carlyle said to Emerson on that memorable day in 1833 when the two sat down in their walk over the Scottish hills, "Christ died on the tree: that built Dunscore kirk yonder: that brought you and me together." The old creeds nursed heroic, God-fearing and God-loving men. True, they sometimes disguised the wolf in sheep's clothing also, but that is the fault of human nature.

Let us be as faithful to our day and generation as our fathers were to theirs. Wendell Phillips said that to be as good as our fathers were, we must be a good deal better. Shall we rail at our Puritan ancestors for the hardness of their creeds? Although the Pauline plan of salvation seems childish to us, it seemed the foundation of the universe for our fathers. To clinch a nail you need something hard, and the Calvinistic creed has clinched the resolution of many a man.

IV. A CHIP FROM THE OLD BLOCK

It makes me more charitable toward my neighbor's creed, childish though I think it is, to remember that it came out of his life, or out of the life around him, as truly as did my own. We cannot separate man, and all that revolves around him, from the totality of things. There is no depravity or cruelty or perversion in the world that is not fed by the life of the world. The war that has depopulated and devastated Europe is just as legitimate a part of total Nature as were all the fruits of the ages of peace and prosperity. Everything in the woods is a part of the woods, and bears their stamp; everything in the sea is a part of the sea. The tumor, the ulcer, and the disease, are a part of our bodies, and are fed by its vitality. In our practical lives we are compelled to separate a part from the whole, to accept this and reject that, but when we essay to comprehend the whole we must see that all are but parts, and that our phi'osophy is lame if it does not see that the so-called good and the so-called bad are fruit of the same tree.

We are prone to separate ourselves from the rest of Nature and to claim for ourselves much that we deny to all other animals, such as the existence of the soul, and its immortality. But we are all of one stuff. Out of the earth has come a creature that has changed the surface of the earth over vast areas; that has changed the course of rivers, and the face of continents; that has harnessed the forces of the earth and turned them against themselves. How the earth elements came to organize themselves into this creature — here we can take no step!

V. A PERSONAL GOD

I once heard an Irish laborer refer solemnly, with an upward lift of the head, to the man up above. He did not refer to the man down below, but no doubt might have done so had occasion required. If we have one, we must have the other to keep the balance. The man up above must keep his skirts clean, and to admit of this the man down below must be the scapegoat.

How long has the belief in the reality of these two manlike beings, the one all good, the other all evil, ruled in the minds and hearts of men! The old Hebrew prophets were drunk with the idea of a manlike Jehovah. A terrible man they made of him — a cruel, despotic ruler, wreaking his vengeance on his enemies, exacting an eye for an eye and a tooth for a tooth, a lover of righteousness, but a vengeful, jealous, angry God. And the man down below was his fit counterpart, blocking and marring or defeating the plans of the man up above. These conceptions go with the infancy of the human reason.

So many phases of our religious belief are the result of imperfect knowledge and false conceptions of the world in which we live! They come down to us from an earlier time, when the earth was regarded as the center of the universe, all other bodies revolving around it. Man lifted his eyes and his hands to heaven in an appeal to the heavenly powers.

It seems as if the religious sense of the mass of mankind was, by the operation of some psychological law, forced to externize and visualize, yes, and humanize, the object upon which its interest centers. Orthodox religion, while proclaiming that God is a spirit, that He is everywhere, that He fills all nature, that not a sparrow falls to the ground without his notice, and that heaven is not a place, but a state of mind, yet makes its God a personal being, endowed with our human attributes, with likes and dislikes, sorely tried by our sins and weaknesses; nearer us sometimes than at others, present everywhere, yet abiding in one particular place called heaven — these and many other childish and contradictory things.

That keen, clear-minded man, Cardinal Newman, regarded God under the image of a maker, detached absolutely like any human workman from the work of his hand. He is the Eternal King, absolutely distinct from the world as being its center, — "Upholder, Governor, and Sovereign Lord." "He created all things out of nothing, and preserves them every moment, and could destroy them as He made them." "He is separated from them by an abyss, and is incommunicable in all his attributes." This being is always described and interpreted in terms of man, or of our own finite human nature, reflecting in his outlines human history, human political and social institutions, and the aims and objects of concrete human beings. He does not hesitate to relate this God to "every movement which has convulsed and refashioned the surface of the earth," and hence to make him responsible for the death and destruction and misery which have attended earthquakes and have set back the tide of human progress. Of course every noxious insect, every noxious plant and beast and death-dealing germ is from Him also. "Wars when just" are from Him also. Who or what are they from when they are not just, the great Cardinal does not say. Can both sides be just? Into such absurdities does the conception of a manlike God lead us.

The modern scientific mind, quite as imaginative — if not more so — as the typical theological mind, never gets mired in such contradictions or tangled up in such childish anthropomorphism. Such confusion arises out of the habit of mind which sees the whole creation directed to man; his good is its one object and aim, and when his good suffers, something has miscarried. The cruel and destructive things in nature can only be accounted for on the theory that some aboriginal calamity, like the fall of man, had visited the world before God took charge of things.

The naturalist sees this as the best possible world, sees that Nature is not an indulgent stepmother, but a strict disciplinarian; that the good and well-being of all is her aim; that suffering and defeat are relative; that God's ways to man are not justified in a day or a week, or in this place or that, but require ages and continents to come to their full fruition. The good and the evil that will come out of the terrible World War will not all be apparent this year, or next, but only in the perspective of history

— in the sum total of human progress of the ages. Such a view is a slap in the face of our egotism which demands instant returns, and which makes the individual supreme.

With Nature, as I have so often said, our standards of good and evil apply to us alone, and they change with the changing years. The naturalist sees that pain and delay and defeat are the price of development; that the world is imperfect, and man is imperfect, because growth and development are the law of nature; that there is always a higher level, and always will be, which we realize only when we look back. A perfect world, as we use the term, would mean the end of all development.

VI. THE ETERNAL

How much is in a name! When we call the power back of all God, it smells of creeds and systems, of superstition, intolerance, persecution; but when we call it Nature, it smells of spring and summer, of green fields and blooming groves, of birds and flowers and sky and stars. I admit that it smells of tornadoes and earthquakes, of jungles and wildernesses, of disease and death, too, but these things make it all the more real to us.

The word "God" has so long stood for the conception of a being who sits apart from Nature, who shapes and rules it as its maker and governor. It is part of the conception of a dual or plural universe,

God and Nature. This offends my sense of the one-ness of creation. It seems to me that there is no other adequate solution of the total problem of life and Nature than what is called "pantheism," which identifies mind and matter, finite and Infinite, and sees in all these diverse manifestations one absolute being. As Emerson truly says, pantheism does not belittle God, it magnifies him. God becomes the one and only ultimate fact that fills the universe and from which we can no more be estranged than we can be estranged from gravitation.

The moment we seek to interpret the Eternal in terms of our own psychology, we get into trouble. We cannot measure the Infinite by the standards of the finite. Our economies, our methods, our aims are not those of Nature. God, in the sense in which I use the term, does not plan and design and adapt means to ends as does man. God is no more the maker than He is the thing made. How natural for us to think that the air was made for us to breathe, the water for us to drink, the light for us to see, and the earth for us to inhabit! But these things are older than we are. I have seen a pumpkin growing in the fence and fitting exactly into the niche amid the rails, but was not the fence there before it was?

There is design in Nature, but not in the sense that there is design in human affairs and contriv-ances. There is no designer. There are living ma-chines, but no machinist. Things grow. Evolution

ACCEPTING THE UNIVERSE

is a vital process. Man's course is a right line, Nature's is a circle. Man aims to cut out the waste, the pain, the failures. How does Nature trim her trees or renew her forests or weed her gardens? Only by a survival of the fittest or the luckiest. Every branch that dies and decays and falls from the tree does so at the risk of the health and well-being of the whole tree. Often the decayed branch leaves a hole that in time causes the death of the tree. See how evenly the pine and spruce and hemlock and oak forests get planted by Nature's haphazard method, but think of the time involved! But what is time to the Eternal? Man cuts out the time and gets his forest quickly. He trims his wood and avoids the danger of delays and decaying wood. He selects such plants for his garden as he desires, and avoids the dangers of the struggle to survive. He takes the side of the weak against the strong, but Nature favors only the strong.

The rain falls upon the just and the unjust. The weather goes its way irrespective of you and me. Storm, tempest, frost, drought, sunshine, are no respecters of persons. The seasons came and went before man appeared, just as they do now. The Eternal never takes sides as man takes sides, but because it does not, should we lose faith? The Eternal takes sides as the sun takes sides, and not otherwise. The light shines for all. Providence is a universal beneficence. The clouds go their way. The

272

beneficence is seen in the slow amelioration of mete-
oric conditions through countless æons, till the cloud
and the bow appeared, and with them conditions
favorable to life. The impartial rains are oblivious
to our human needs, but, as I so often say, they are
on the side of life. They are on the side of development. They made the sublime drama of evolution
possible.

The weather favored us æons before we were born,
because it favored life. Therefore, when we say that
the Eternal is neither for us nor against us, we
mean in our special human sense. He is on the side
of the righteous only when the righteous live according to the rule of Nature or rightness, or in
harmony with the eternal order. And he is against
the unrighteous when they transgress this order. In
vain do we pray for victory on the eve of battle,
except in so far as prayer puts courage into our
hearts. Victory is for him who marshals the physical
and moral forces the most skillfully. The victory is
from the Eternal whoever wins, because it is the
fruit of the order which It established, or, rather,
which It is.

As we cannot get away from Nature, we cannot
get away from the Eternal. He sticketh closer than
a brother, closer than the blood in our own hearts,
not always to bless and to cheer, often to hinder and
depress. Not all ease and joy is life; it is as often
struggle, tears, defeat.

ACCEPTING THE UNIVERSE

Not by placing God afar off in the heavens — a supersensuous, supermundane, supernatural being — do we make the problem easier. Not till we bring Him down to earth and incarnate Him (the old myth of Christ again), and identify Him with everything without us and within — not till God becomes man — do we see a light under the feet of Fate; not till then do we see love and fatherhood and brotherhood and sacrifice and humility and beneficence and altruism in Nature. When we see man as a part of Nature, we see him as a part of God.

In humanity alone do we see the face of justice, of mercy, of charity, of forgiveness, of reverence, of renunciation — human virtues, they, too, come out of the heart of Nature. If this is a hard gospel, still it is tangible, real, livable. We cannot live other than on familiar terms with Nature. In her we see the sources of our power, our help, our health. We know the conditions of our well-being. We know the price we have to pay for each blessing. Our reason, our intelligence, we come by honestly and inevitably. Their fountainhead is in Nature.

Amid the agony and turmoil of war we need not lose faith. We know that Nature is still Nature. If disease and pestilence and famine rage, we know that there are weapons with which to fight them. We know that order comes out of chaos, that life comes out of death. We have neither to curse our gods nor to praise them, neither to do penance nor to offer burnt offerings, but only to take and use wisely the gifts they bestow.

VII. AN IMPARTIAL DEITY

WHAT difficulties and contradictions we fall into the moment we identify Nature with God, and what equal or greater difficulties we fall into if we refuse to identify Nature with God! True it is that in the former case we bring God very near and make him very real; we see and feel our direct and continuous dependence upon Him — indeed, that we are a part of Him; that every breath we draw, and every thought we think, and every pound of energy we put forth is in and through Him; and that we can no more wander or escape from Him than we can escape gravity or chemical affinity. There are no skeptics or atheists in regard to Nature. It alone exists and goes on forever. But here comes the pinch! God as Nature is not only the author of the good, He is the author of what we call evil also; He is as many-sided as Nature is. The savage and merciless aspects of Nature are of Him also; He is in the jungles of Africa, as well as in the walks of culture and refinement; in the destroying tornado as well as in the gentle summer breeze; in the overwhelming floods as well as in the morning dews. He is as much the author of disease as He is of health; of war, pestilence, famine, as He is of peace, plenty, and the progress of the world. He is in the trenches and the slaughter of the contending armies as truly as in the most peaceful and pious family or social circle in the world. The asphyxiating gases are his, and the bursting bombs, no less than the breaking hearts and the prayerful souls at home. The comets that come like apparitions in the heavens, and then are gone, and the stars that shine steadfastly, are all a part of the same scheme. The dragons and monsters that possessed the earth and the fruits thereof for millions of years in geologic time were the work of that divinity which shapes our ends to-day.

We separate ourselves from Nature and flatter ourselves that we belong to another and higher order; that we alone are of divine origin, and not involved in the fate of the rest of Creation; but we are fragments of the same granite that forms the foundation of the earth. "I am stuccoed with birds and quadrupeds all over," says Whitman. The reptile was our ancestor; we were cradled in the old seas; we are kin to the worm and the mollusk; we derive from creeping, swimming, noisome things, from the slime and mud of the old sea bottoms, from the cosmic dust and the solar radiations. Why should we put on superior airs when not one atom of matter will turn aside for us, not one law of physics cease to operate to save us from destruction? The vast army of elemental forces knows us not. We may divert them and bend them to our will, but they heed us not; they destroy us the moment we lose control.

Nature does not love us any more than she hates us; she goes her way, indifferent.

The best we can say about it all is that Nature, or the Natural Providence, is too big for us to grasp; that in these seas we can find no soundings. But we are here, the world is beautiful, life is worth living, love always pays; Nature serves us when we know how to use her; when we plant and sow wisely God will send the increase. Friendly or unfriendly, of God or of the Devil, the physical forces have ministered to us. More things have been for us than have been against us; more winds have blown our barks into safe harbors than have dashed us upon the rocks. There are more refreshing showers than devastating tornadoes; more sunshine than forked lightning; more fertile land upon the earth than parched deserts; a broader belt of genial climates than of frigid zones. Thorns and spines and nettles are the exception in vegetation; stings and venomous fangs are the exception in animal life. Hawks can catch the smaller birds, yet there are vastly more small birds than hawks. The weasel can catch the rabbit and the squirrel and the rat, yet there are ten-fold, fifty-fold, more of these rodents than there are weasels. The carnivorous beasts of the plains and of the jungle do not exterminate the herbivorous; there is more good than evil everywhere; more peace than war; more kindness than cruelty. The God of Nature goes his way, but his way is our way; we have arisen out of Nature; as it is, the chances of life have been in our favor; the stream makes its own channel; the waters find their way to the sea; they do not all stagnate on the way. Some of the seed which the winds sow falls upon barren places, but not the most of it. Some men are born criminals or cripples or malformed, but not the majority. The creatures preyed upon always vastly outnumber the creatures that prey upon them. And in truth, in the whole realm of Nature more things wait upon man than war upon him.

VIII. FINITE AND INFINITE

THE unnamable, the unthinkable, the omnipotent, the omnipresent, we cannot discuss or define in terms of our humanity. The moment we try to do so we are involved in contradictions, just as we are when we try to define the sphere in terms of the plane. The sphere has no length, it has no breadth, it has no thickness, in the sense that bodies upon its surface have. It has no weight, and it has no beginning and no end, and we may say that its motion is eternal rest; yet rest implies motion, and motion implies rest.

When we say that there is no God, we only mean

that there is no being that we can define or conceive of in terms of man. Nothing in the finite can help us in dealing with the infinite. The Infinite, the Omnipotent, the Omnipresent, cannot be a being without sharing the limitations of being, or without being subject to the bounds of time and space. If God is everywhere, He is nowhere; if He is all-powerful, his power has no contrary, and hence ceases to exist. One after another the human and personal attributes we ascribe to Him disappear when we try to conceive of Him in terms of the infinite. The infinite is equivalent to negation. There are no terms in which we can define the ether; it is the negative of all things that have length and breadth and thickness, or motion or rest or substance, or friction or cohesion, or place or power. An infinite being is as much a contradiction of terms as a square or plane sphere would be. If God is a person, with human-like attributes and emotions, — though we call them divine, — it is legitimate to ask, Where is He? where was He before the solar systems took form? where will He be after they have again become formless?

Our inevitable anthropomorphism prefigures the Infinite as superman; He is man magnified to infinity. He is the supreme king or ruler of the universe. We dream of seeing Him face to face; He has eyes, ears, hands, feet, and the emotions of love, anger, pity, and the like. Man thus imposes his own form upon the power that is and upholds the cosmos. He carves it into his own image, and then seeks to propitiate it and influence it as He Himself is propitiated and influenced. Praise is sweet to it, honor is sweet, revenge is sweet, because these things are sweet to man.

When we call this force Nature, we bring it near to us and can see and feel our direct relation to it. We are bone of its bone and flesh of its flesh. We see its impersonal or unpersonal character. We get light on the vexed problem of good and evil which is such an insoluble enigma to the theologians.

Nature embraces all; she fathers and mothers all; has no partialities, knows no exceptions, no miracles, no deputied atonements, no evil apart from the good and no good apart from the evil, no life without death and no death without life.

IX. THE INSOLUBLE

WHAT desperate efforts mankind has made to shape this vast, blind, unconscionable power we call Nature into an image of a God that would satisfy our moral and spiritual wants and aspirations! Where did men get their standards of such a God? They have evidently been slowly evolved through the friction of man with man. They have possessed survival value. Love, truth, justice, mercy, have contributed to the fullness of life and to length of days. One may adopt Biblical language and say that righteousness endureth forever. The triumph of the wicked is only for a season; it may be a long season, it may embrace whole periods of human history, and entail measureless suffering on the human race, but change and retribution surely come. The way of man's moral and material progress is like the stream that now hurries, now tarries, is now disrupted and noisy in rapids and falls, now sluggish and almost stagnant in long level reaches, but which does go forward and reach its goal at last. But is there not some predetermined bent toward righteousness, — not of the ecclesiastical sort, but of the scientific sort, — toward the relations of man with man, that results in the greatest good to the greatest number, — a bent inherent in the nature of things? Would evolution have taken the road toward man and all the other forms of life blindly, accidentally? Would it have started at all had there not been some initial impulse, or some thought, somewhere, of all that was to follow?

The doctrine of design does not meet the problem; the doctrine of chance does not meet it. Design in our human world means a designer. What, then, does it mean in the non-human world? There can be no design in such a world, because the human mind is not present. There can be no chance, because a chance jumbling and collision of the primordial elements could not result in the organized matter

that is life, any more than a thousand of brick
dumped upon the ground can take the form of a
house. The brick and mortar demand an architect,
and organized matter demands an organizing principle. Whence its source? There we are where no
further step can be taken. What about the divine
mind? But that is jumping the whole question. If
you place your God here, I shall ask him some embarrassing questions, such as, Where did you come
from? Where have you been all these æons? Why
are you so wasteful and dilatory in your methods?
Why have you made the world so full of misery?
Or, I might ask the question a little boy asked his
father: "Why did God make Satan?" The problem, it seems to me, is quite as embarrassing to us
mortals with a God as without one. It is just as hard
to account for a God as to account for the initial impulse. In both cases we have in our hands a rope
with only one end. In trying to find the other end,
we only get ourselves hopelessly tied up.

X. PAYING THE DEBT

IN my youth I often heard the old people speak of
death as "paying the debt of Nature" — "He has
paid the debt." Life puts us in debt to Nature —
the earth, the air, the water — for the elements of
our bodies and the powers of our minds, and the
time inevitably comes when we must settle the account. That we are going to have something left

over — that we have only to pay the debt of the body, and not of the mind — is one of the dreams that it is hard for most persons to give up. Will not then the universal mind that pervades Nature claim its own also? Can you and I hope to remain detached from it forever? Is that a consummation devoutly to be wished?

Be assured that no particle of soul or body can be lost. But processes may cease; the flame of the lamp may go out, and the sum total of force and matter remain the same. When a blade of grass dies, a process has ended, and as mysterious a process as went on in Cæsar's brain and body. And when all life on the earth and in our universe ceases, if it ever does, the problem would remain just as puzzling, if we can fancy ourselves still here to puzzle over it. We are links in an endless cycle of change in which we cannot separate the material from what we call the spiritual.

The water in our bodies to-day may have flashed as a dewdrop yesterday, or lent itself to the splendor of the sunrise or sunset, or played a part in the bow in the clouds. To-morrow it may be whirling in the vortex of a tornado, or helping to quench the life of a drowning man, or glistening in the frost figures on the window-pane. The movements of the brain molecules in which the phenomena of thought and consciousness are so mysteriously involved, they, too, are links in the cycle of change.

. One of our younger poets, John Russell Mc-
Carthy, has had the courage to say:

> "that we must look for life
> Hereafter, not by one and one, — your soul
> Alone among the souls of other men,
> Drifting and staying, a thing apart forever —
> But we must see when all at last is counted
> And the great sum is made, how one by one
> We have returned to Her, the Mother of All, —
> The bit of soul-stuff that She loaned us.
>
> For we must live at last a part of Her —
> For we shall be forever as one with Her."

The reverent old people to whom I just referred
paid the debt long ago, and the day of reckoning for
some of us cannot be far off. After the account is
closed who or what has profited by the transaction?
We are prone to put such questions to Nature, but
they are irrelevant. The universe is not run for
profit, as we use the term. So far as we can see, it is
run just to satisfy the æsthetic and creative feeling
of the Eternal. When the sidereal systems in space
run down, they are wound up again, and suns and
planets are started anew. The great game never
comes to an end; in fact, it is unthinkable that it
should ever have begun, except as the flowers begin
in spring, or as a man begins when he is born. Antecedents! Antecedents! — always. We cannot apply
our standards of loss and gain to the dealings of
the Eternal with us. "That I have positively appeared," says Whitman, "that is enough."

Each of us is an incarnation of the universal mind, as is every beast of the field and jungle, and every fowl of the air, and every insect that creeps and flies; and we can only look upon creation as an end in itself. To ask what the great spectacle is for, is to betray our tradesman habit of mind. Man is a link in an endless chain of being. If we ask what he is for, the old answer of the catechism is as good as any — "To glorify God and enjoy Him forever." In other words, to make the most of his life and strive for the highest happiness, which is knowledge and appreciation of the universal. Coleridge says we glorify God when we work for the well-being of mankind.

How quite impossible it is for us to adjust our minds to the thought of death — to the thought of the absolute negation of life! When we torment ourselves about death, about the coldness and darkness of the grave, about being cut off from all the warm and happy currents of life that flow about us, we are unconsciously thinking of ourselves as still living, or as conscious of the gloom and negation that await us. Thus, when Huxley wrote to a friend (John Morley) that the thought of extinction disturbed him more and more as he neared the end of life, he fell into this common fallacy, or contradiction. "It flashes across me," he writes, "at all sorts of times with a sort of horror that in 1900 I shall probably know no more of what is going on than I did in

1800. I had sooner be in hell, a good deal —" as if he expected to lie awake nights in his grave lamenting his sad fate and saying to himself, "I had sooner be in hell," where also he expected he would be conscious of his improved condition!

What possible difference could it make to him if he did not know any more in 1900 than he did in 1800? Did he expect to enjoy his knowledge in 1900? If not, why worry about it? What he was really lamenting was that he did not know then and there what he might know if he lived till 1900. He knew that human knowledge was making tremendous strides, and the thought that he should not share in its advancement chilled him.

It is all very human, but very childish. We may to-day dread some task or ordeal that we are to face to-morrow, because to-morrow we expect to be alive, but shall we shrink from the to-morrow of death on the same grounds?

There is wisdom as well as wit in the epitaph in dialogue which a clever Greek Byzantine composed for Pyrrho:

"Art thou dead, Pyrrho?"

"I do not know."

If we put the same question to our own dead, if they could answer, they would say, "We do not know." If they knew, would not that be proof that they were not dead? May we not answer Huxley that if consciousness is extinguished with life, he is not going to lie awake nights in his grave worrying about it? There is comfort in the thought that if there is no immortality, we shall not know it.

Rereading that wise and delightful old Frenchman, Montaigne, I find that more than three hundred years ago he was of the same mind that I am in this matter: "Why should we fear a thing whose being lost cannot be lamented?" "To lament that we shall not be alive a hundred years hence is the same folly as to be sorry we were not alive a hundred years ago."

An avaricious man might worry if he knew he would have no more money on the next Christmas than he had on the last, unless his physician had assured him that he could not be alive on the next Christmas. Then, if he worried, it would be on account of his heirs. But one's heirs cannot inherit his wisdom; it dies with him.

Death is such an extraordinary, such an unspeakable event that we cannot think of ourselves as non-existent. When you try to see yourself in your own coffin, or standing beside your own grave, it is still as a living man that you thus behold yourself. It is, of course, as living men and women that we are disturbed over thoughts of the grave. The future is just as secure for us all as is the past. A moment between two eternities is life; a spark that draws a brief line upon the darkness and is gone. The spark has its antecedent condition in the wood and coal and the processes of combustion from which it sprang, and it has its subsequent conditions in the invisible gases into which it has vanished, but as a point of heat and light, it exists no more. Our wise attitude toward death is, I think, to forget or ignore it entirely. We shall not know it when it overtakes us. "*Avida nunquam desinere mortalitas.*" "Men must endure their going hence, even as their coming hither — ripeness is all."

XI. DEATH

I

IN death the elements of the body are not changed — oxygen is still oxygen, carbon still carbon. What has happened, then? Can it be explained by saying that a process has been reversed? Does it bear any true analogy to the redistribution of type after the printer has set it up and printed his book? The type is the same, but the relation of all the units has been changed. The printer has arranged them so that collectively they expressed to him certain meanings or ideas. These ideas did not exist in the type, but in the order of its arrangement. In one order or combination the letters meant one thing; in another order or combination they expressed quite another. The same type will spell dog or God. When redistributed and returned to the different fonts, the letters express nothing but themselves. If this is a true analogy, then, in the case of the living book, man, what stands for the compositor and printer? We can only call the compositor the organizing impulse; but whence this impulse, and whose idea is it trying to express? The redistribution of the elements of the body is done through the activity of other forms of life — the micro-organisms — those minute forms reduce the body to its original elements. As we thus have life at the end of the life of an organism, do we also have life at the beginning of the organism? Ancestral life certainly, or the primordial germ; but is there a living principle back of and before all? Does the logic of the situation force us to the belief in an original Creator? The human mind is so constituted that in some form or under definite concepts, we have to postulate a first or primal Cause; we have to think of a beginning; but is there any beginning to a circle, or any center to the surface of a sphere? There may be no beginning or no limit in time or space to the cosmos. This is unthinkable to us in our present state. Yet in making that statement I am thinking of the unthinkable. We can deal only with parts of Nature; as a whole it is beyond our power to grasp. All bodies on the earth's surface unsupported fall; this is our universal experience. All moving bodies come to a standstill unless power from without is constantly supplied. Perpetual motion is impossible, but the earth and the other planets are unsupported, and their motion is perpetual. Or we may say that they fall forever toward the sun and never reach it, and that the sun falls forever toward some other sun or system and never reaches it. The laws of force and matter as we contend with them in our experiences are inoperative in sidereal space; there is motion without friction, energy without waste, dissipation without exhaustion. Neither upper nor under, neither falling nor rising, neither end nor beginning. Cause and effect, rest and motion, are one. The self-activity of the universe quite transcends our experiences; the self-maintenance of living bodies is far beyond our reach; any end to the chain of causal sequence is quite unthinkable to us. Our minds are made in that way. They are fashioned in the school of cause and effect.

Nothing can get out of the universe because there is no out to the universe. Can that which has no ending have a beginning? Can that which has no circumference have a center? Can we think of anything so hot that it could not be hotter? Or so small that it could not be smaller? Or so big that it could not be bigger? No, because our minds have been schooled in this comparative method. Our sense shows us a world of degrees. We can think of absolute darkness, but not of absolute light. In the Mammoth Cave you may realize absolute darkness; but even on the sun itself would you experience absolute light? We seem to be able to find an end to the negative, but not to the positive. We can think of a body as at absolute rest, but can we conceive of it going so fast that it could not go faster?

Death is our consciousness of a peculiar change in matter, just as life is our consciousness of the opposite change — one destructive, the other constructive. The constituents of the body remain unchanged, but a peculiar activity set up among the particles, by what, we know not, is instituted in life and ceases in death. An organism is made up of organs, all working together, but each subordinated to the whole. The whole, this concerted action, may cease, and the individual dies, as we say, and yet the minute subdivisions, the cells, may be alive. Certain ferments in the body may go on for some time after the life of the man has gone out. And living cells may go on multiplying endlessly without producing an organized being.

II

"It is all right," said Walt Whitman to me as I was leaving his death-bed and hearing his voice for the last time — "It is all right." Of course it was all right, and it will be all right when each and all of us fall into the last eternal sleep. Else it would not be. Our being here is all right, is it not? "Friendly and faithful," says Whitman, "are the arms that have helped me," and friendly and faithful must be the arms that bear us away. If it was good to come, it will be good to go — good in the large, cosmic sense,

good in that it is in keeping with the spirit of the All.
Not the good of our brief personal successes and
triumphs, but good as evolution is good, as the processes of growth and decay are good. If life is good,
death must be equally good, as each waits upon the
other. From what point of view can we say that
death is not all right? Certainly not from the point
of view of this universe. Archimedes could have
moved the world had he had some other world upon
which to place his lever, and we must have some
other universe to plant our feet upon to condemn
death.

As I have already said, we look upon death as
an evil because we look upon it from the happy
fields of life, and see ourselves as alive in our
graves and lamenting that we are shut off from all
the light and love and movement of the world.
Does our prenatal state seem an evil?

Did anything begin *de novo*, when we came into
being? Not the elements of our bodies surely; they
were as old as the cosmos; not the germ of our minds
and souls; they were as old as the human race and
older — old as the first dawn of life. Is it the *I* that
is new? — that which makes you you and me me?
And that is probably nothing more than a new distribution and arrangement of the physical and psychical elements and forces of which and by which
we are made. The pattern of our personality is new;
each of us differs somewhat from all the myriads of

human beings who have lived upon the earth; but is form, pattern, personality, separable from the material that composes it?)

It may be cheerfully admitted that when we look at the question in this light, we are whistling to keep our courage up. What of it? The band plays to keep the courage of the soldiers up when they go into battle, and what are we but soldiers fighting the good fight of truth against error, of courage against fear, of the heroic against the pusillanimous? The whole is greater than any of its parts. Nature is more than man. We must learn to efface ourselves. The soul knows no rewards or punishments. If it be heroic to sacrifice life in this world, it may be equally heroic to sacrifice life in any other world, so that we prove ourselves worthy of the gods.

XII. HEAVEN AND EARTH

TRULY things are not what they seem. When we put heaven and earth far apart, we think as children. Heaven and earth are pretty close together. The shortest arm can reach from one to the other. When we go to heaven we shall not have far to travel, and I dare say the other place is quite as near, and, if reports be true, the road is broader and easier to travel. What children we are in such matters! The wisest men have the language of ignorance and superstition imposed upon them. How difficult it is not to think of the heavens up there as a reality, something above us and superior to us, a finer world, nearer God, lighted by the stars, the abode of spirits, the source of all good, our final celestial home. Did not Elijah ascend into heaven? Did not Paul have heavenly visions? Have not the saints in all ages turned their faces and lifted imploring hands to heaven? How these things have burnt themselves into our minds! We cannot escape them.

In our floods of religious emotion we instinctively look away from the earth. The mystery, the immensity, the purity of the heavens above us make us turn our faces thitherward, and as naturally make us turn downward when we consider the source of evil. The poor old earth which has mothered us and nursed us we treat with scant respect. Our awe and veneration we reserve for the worlds we know not of. Our senses sell us out. The mud on our shoes disenchants us. It is only Whitman with his cosmic consciousness that can closely relate the heavens and the earth:

> "Underneath the divine soil,
> Overhead the sun."

To most of us the morning stars that once sang together are of another stuff. The music of the spheres must be vastly different from the roar and grind of our old rusty and outworn planet. So we turn to the heavens, the abode of purity and light. So do we discount and black-list the earth where we have to pay in struggle and pain the price of our development. Think you we should not have to pay the same price in any other world worth living in?

Emerson in his Journal quotes his brother Charles as saying long ago that "the nap was worn off the earth"; it was become threadbare, like an outworn garment. Probably it seems so to each of us as time goes on. In places in Europe the nap must be very short at this time. But the nap will come again, even on those shell-swept regions, after Nature has had her way. Nature grows old in geologic or in cosmic time; the mountains decay, the waters recede; but in man's time the earth is endowed with perennial youth.

Science strips us of our illusions and delusions; it strips us of most of the garments in which the spirit of man has sought in all ages to clothe itself against the chill of an impersonal universe; it takes down the protecting roof of the heavens above us and shows us an unspeakable void strewn with suns and worlds beyond numbers to compute, but nowhere any signs of the blessed abode to which our religious aspirations have pointed.

It is interesting, in this connection, to note the attitude of the old writers, such as Cornaro, the Italian, toward the heavens. They evidently look upon the heavens as outside of Nature. In speculating as to why it is that some persons have so little vitality, Cornaro reckons the influence of the heavens may be one cause. He says he never could persuade himself to believe that Nature, being the mother of all, could be so ungenerous to any of her children; hence it must be some hostile influence from above. Similar notions seem to have been held in Shakespeare's time:

> "It is the stars,
> The stars above us, govern our conditions;
> Else one self mate and make could not beget
> Such different issues."

XIII. THINKING AND ACTING

IT is true we do not, as a rule, act without thinking, or without some sort of psychic process, but thinking and acting are radically different. Or, we may say that the practical reason is alone concerned in action, and the abstract intellect in general reasoning. When we come to act, we know that we are free to choose between two or more objects or courses; when we think or reason abstractly, we know the will is not free. Every act has its antecedent cause. But we are practically free because we feel no restraint or compulsion. We feel responsible for our acts. We do not blame our red-haired father, or our grandfather of Irish blood, for our hasty temper; we feel that this is our very selves. What we call moral responsibility rests upon this sense of freedom. We are not aware of the fatality that binds us, any more than we are of the weight of the atmosphere that presses upon us so tremendously. At the court of absolute reason we see what puppets and automata we are, but at the court of practical justice we see and feel that we are free to do right as we see the right. The contradictions which Balfour sees, in his chapter on "Naturalism and Ethics," between the results of practical life and of abstract reasoning is of a kind which one sees everywhere in the universe. The circle is a perpetual contradiction. How can a line go in all directions? — and in no direction? In our practical lives there is an upper and an under, an up and a down, but away from the earth, or considering the earth as a whole, there is no such thing.

Righteous indignation at the misconduct of others, or self-condemnation, repentance, remorse, are reasonable feelings because we actually feel them. We have no choice in the matter. To whatever conclusion abstract reason leads us in regard to them, it does not affect our practical conduct, because our conduct is founded upon the sense of freedom. We are here to act, to do, and not to reason abstractly. This is the tree of the forbidden fruit. When we eat of it we know things that may stand in the way of our practical living. Balfour should see that we are determinists or naturists when we reason, but free agents when we act, and that there is no getting away from the contradiction.

I may be the duplicate of my father, or of my grandfather; every one of my traits may be inherited; but that does not prevent me from feeling that they are my own; they are vital in me as they were in him, and I feel responsible for my own acts just as he did for his, though I could not act otherwise. I could not, but I did not know it. I thought I could act as I pleased.

The world which philosophy reveals to us is vastly different from the world practical life reveals. We are sure that light and sound are real entities, but philosophy tells us that one is the sensation which vibrations in the ether, set going by the sun, make upon the optic nerve, and that sound is the sensation which vibrations in the air make upon the auditory nerve. When we know this we do not change our action in reference to them — they are still just as real to our senses as ever they were. The moral law is not discredited or overthrown when we discover through the abstract reason that fate, or necessity, rules our lives. We made the moral law and we try to live up to it. We do not always succeed. All trees aim at the vertical position; it is the position which gravity imposes upon them; but owing to various accidents and conditions the trees are not all plumb. How free they seem to grow at almost any angle with the plane of the earth's surface! How they run out their branches horizontally in defiance of the gravity that rules them and lift up in their trunks and leaves tons of water and other minerals against the pull of gravity! How free they

seem, how they bend to the wind that would overthrow them, how various they are in form and habit
of growth, in the shape of their leaves, the kinds of
their fruits, the character of their roots! Yet science
shows us how the unalterable physical laws rule
them. They lean toward the light and the free air in
obedience to physical and chemical laws. And yet,
no doubt, if the trees were conscious of themselves,
as we are, every oak-tree would say, "I feel free to
be an oak," and every pine-tree and beech and willow and maple would feel a like freedom. The Irishman feels no compulsion or necessity in being an
Irishman, nor the Frenchman in being a Frenchman. All life is held in the leash of physical and
chemical laws, and yet knows it not.

We feel that there is beauty in nature; when we
reflect, we know that the feeling for beauty is an
emotion of our own minds, and not a quality of outward things. Scenes radically different awaken the
emotion in us, or may awaken it in one and not in
another (see Emerson's ecstasy on a bare moor).
The world is what we make it, and duty is what we
make it, and the ugly is what we make it. Putrefac-
tion, repulsive to us, is to science a beautiful chemical process. Odors that are offensive to us are evidently agreeable to the dog. Sounds which please us
seem to disturb him. The absolute is outside of life.
If the orbs of the heavens were conscious, they
would doubtless feel free to go where they do go; it

would be their choice; it would pain them to do otherwise. The comet rushes toward the sun with joy; the music of the spheres is the expression of their freedom and contentment. Can you help winking when the flashlight goes off, or when a missile passes near your eyes? Our voluntary actions are equally based upon physical laws.

Balfour, in his "Foundation of Belief," talks about the beauty of holiness, the beauty of sanctity, but these things are beautiful only to a certain type of mind. The time will come when they will not be looked upon as beautiful or desirable. These conceptions grew when men lived for another world, when this world stood to them as the sum of evil. Men then saw nothing holy or divine on earth except the denying of earth. That state of mind has largely passed. Holy men have had their day. We see now that this world is a celestial body, and that all our conceptions of heavenly abodes are untenable. For my part the most lovable and admirable men and women I have known had no savor of sanctity. They were wise, kind, helpful, loving, living with zest the life of every day, intent on making their earthly lives square with what is generally accepted as right conduct, and therefore comfortably indifferent to what the theologians are so concerned about — salvation after death, and the securing of their "mansions in the skies." Martyrdom bravely faced excites our admiration, all heroic acts are beautiful and admirable, and there are good naturalistic reasons why this should be so. But our religious history has begotten a whole brood of ideas that must gradually fade and go out, and our standards will more and more be those of this world.

Mr. Balfour would hardly deny that the organ with which we do our thinking and reasoning and form our deductions, the organ which is the seat of our emotions of the beautiful and of religious aspirations, is a mass of gray and white matter, and that all these things are the result of certain molecular changes or movements in the fluids or solids of the brain substance ; in other words, that there is a physical and physiological basis to all our mental and emotional life. Does this material side in any way discredit these faculties and feelings? Does not all that we call the spiritual adhere in the material? Can we find that inner world, or any clue to it, by dissecting the brain? Has it, therefore, any reality except in our imagination? Prove that it exists apart from or independent of the body, and there is no more to be said.

But what I wanted most to say is that the reason of things, or final explanation of things seems to take the poetry and romance out of them. Reduce religion or æsthetics or art to terms of psychology, and they no longer appeal to the emotions or stimulate the imagination. Naturalism is true — reason can reach no other conclusion — but the truths of naturalism do not satisfy the moral and religious nature.

The heart is a big, strong, self-acting, muscular pump, but when we lay our hand upon the heart and refer our emotions, our love, our aspirations, to it, we idealize it, we do not then think of its physical function and character. By this act we are still deferring to the ancient and outworn belief that in this region resides the soul — the part of man that loves and hates and hopes and fears.

The brain is the temple of the mind or the vestibule of the spiritual world, but we can explain it only in terms of anatomy, physiology, and physics which darken and chill our sensibilities.

Things and movements come about through natural processes, not through supernatural ones, but when we state these processes in the only terms in which they can be stated, the religious soul feels hurt and orphaned. All our religious or theological explanations of things discredit matter and the material world, discredit Nature and all her processes. Evolution is anti-religious; that man is of animal origin is still a hard doctrine to the old-fashioned theologian. Why is it not equally a hard doctrine to him that we were ever babies or embryos, carried about and associated with the viscera of our mothers' bodies? We have got to exalt the natural, the material, and free our minds from the illusions of the old theologies before we can see the truth and beauty of naturalism. The sacred, the celestial, the divine, the holy, all are terms that date from a pre-scientific age, before man's relation to the universe was understood. They are significant only in reference to another world and another life of an entirely different order.

The eternal, immutable moral law to which Balfour refers, what is it? Who instituted it? Is it other than the law of right and wrong which mankind is coming more and more clearly to see, and more and more fully to value in the course of evolution? You may set the seal of some hypothetical, supernatural power upon it, but what about supernatural powers in a universe governed by natural laws? The religious enthusiasm of the race, the saints, the devotees, the so-called holy ones, have doubtless had their value; they have helped lubricate the grinding machinery of life; but their day is at an end. We must invest our fund of love, our veneration, our heroism, our martyrdom in this world, and not look to the next.

That Nature is irrational, unhuman, no one can deny, not because she is less, but because she is more; she is above reason, above man. Our reason calls Nature irrational because the reason is a special faculty, and is limited; it takes in the arc, so to speak, but not the full circle. Nature is irrational, not because she is not suffused with mind, but because she does not count the cost, because our economies do not fit her especial scheme. Life is synonymous with intelligence; all organic nature shows the working of the primal mind — the adaptation of means to specific ends, and the steady improvement from lower to higher.

What we think, when trying to render an account to the reason of the enigma of life, often has little relation to what we do, as practical, struggling beings. We are free to think in all directions, free to move in but few. Our thoughts are like the vapors that drift with the winds, or that expand equally in all directions. Our actual lives are like the waters that must flow in definite channels, and turn some wheel or irrigate some tract of land, or quench some creature's thirst. That naturalism, with minds which take an interest in it, should result in low standards of life, or in any form of disorder or failure, I do not believe. Only clear, strong, truth-loving spirits can accept this explanation of things. Much more mentality is demanded than is demanded by the old conceptions. Hence one has to face the terrible realities and discipline the spirit to accept them. In the old views, in supernaturalism, all this is done for one by the Church and one is a member of a personally conducted party to heaven.

XIV. THE TIDE OF LIFE

WE cannot find God by thinking. Thinking starts us on an endless quest. We can find neither end nor beginning to the sequence of cause and effect. It is a circle that ends and begins forever in itself. Men find what they call God in action, in experience, because in these practical dealings with the forces of this world they are under the law of cause and effect. They find beginnings and endings, they find an upper and an under side, they find a lower and a higher, a greater and a smaller: but in thought all things are relative. Some wise man has said that if there were no God, we should have to invent one — invent one if we wish to explain the world in the terms of human experience. Thinking turns the world topsy-turvy.

Our religious natures are still Ptolemaic. The heavens still revolve around us. We do not with the eye of the flesh see ourselves in this world as on a sphere — on a celestial body floating in space; we see ourselves as on an endless plain over and under which the heavenly bodies pass. It is only with the eye of the mind that we see things in their true relation and see that there is no up and no down, no under and no over, apart from the earth, and no God who rules as a ruler rules. We do not gain the tremendous facts of astronomy through our everyday experience; our search after scientific truth reveals them to us. Through this inquiry we see the grand voyage we are making among the stars, and see that the heavens are not a realm apart from us, the abode of superior beings, but are our veritable habitat; that our earth is a celestial body among myriads of others, and that when we solemnly lift our eyes heavenward, we are lifting them to other worlds made of the same stuff as our own. Our religious emotions and aspirations lead us to look away from the earth and to imagine finer and fairer realms, but disinterested science does not humor our illusions; it brings us back to earth again, back to the heaven we despise. Hence the trouble the narrow religious nature has with science. It experiences a cold shudder before its revelations and will none of it. It will have beginnings and endings, boundaries and limitations, heavenly and earthly, and will read the impersonal laws of the universe in terms of our personal human needs and relations. It sets up a judge and ruler of creation modeled on our human plan, and then to get out of the dilemma in which it finds itself, with all the sin and misery and injustice of the world which it finds upon its hands, and which omnipotent love and mercy could never tolerate, dopes itself with theological casuistry that seeks to justify the ways of God to man. It is a world-old problem. The only way I see out of it is by purging our minds of the old dogmas and boldly facing the reality as science shows it to us. Religion as the world has so long used the term — that human mixture of fear, reverence, superstition, and selfish desire — has had its day. We may still marvel and love and admire and rejoice, but let us fear and plead and tremble no more. There is nothing to be afraid of worse than ourselves, and nothing to implore and propitiate farther removed from us than the rain and the sunshine. In the end all things work together for our good — not always for the good of to-day, or of to-morrow, or for this man or that man, but for the good of all, for the good which evolution brings in its train. Evolution brings what we call evil also, but evil is a term of our human experience, and the Infinite, the Eternal, knows it not. What is evil to one creature in the struggle for life we have seen to be good to another, and often what our religious fears recoil from, science sees as the beneficent operation of law. In Nature nothing is unclean; her chemistry meets and appropriates all, even when we flee or faint. Our physical well-being forces upon us the conception of the clean and the unclean, but in the processes of the Nature that sustains us both are one.

We are adjustable creatures. We are neither sugar nor salt, neither round nor square, neither iron nor lead; we yield and we resist, we melt and we freeze. We are as adjustable and as adaptive as the leaves of the forest. The firmly woven texture of the leaf, its mobile stem, the flexible branch to which it clings, make it secure against the ordinary vicissitudes to which it is subject.

Man is the most adaptive of all creatures; he is

as local as the turtle, and as cosmopolitan as the eagle. All climes, all conditions of wet and dry, of plain and mountain, of sea and shore, of island and continent, are his. His home is the world. Lately he has conquered the air with forces of the earth. Will he yet conquer the ether with forces of the air? Already the ether conveys his messages, but no mechanical contrivance of his can yet lay hands upon it.

Let me again say that by the Natural Providence I mean the general beneficence of Nature, the blind, undiscriminating, uncalculating, inevitable beneficence which brought us here and keeps us here, and makes it good for us to be alive, despite the vicissitudes and the occasional apparently lesser phases of malevolence to which we are subject. The changing seasons, the fertile soils, the rains, the dews, the snows, the blue skies, the green earth, the flowing streams, the gentle winds, in fact all the conditions that make life possible and permanent, are expressions of this beneficence. The whole movement of evolution, with all its dark and forbidding phases, is an expression of it. Allow time enough and the turbid stream flows itself clear, and the stream of evolution is fast losing, has lost, most of its terrible and repellent features. At its flood, in earlier geologic times, one may say that its waters were charged with the elements of huge, uncouth, and terrible forms which have been mostly eliminated; the current has cleared and purified as it advanced; the dragons and monsters have nearly disappeared; the reptiles have receded and left the fowl and birds; the saurians are gone, and in their stead we have the more comely and useful forms of mammalian life. From our human point of view — and we can have no other — creation has refined. The tide of life is still like a river that has its noisome and unlovely margins, but how has it cleared and sweetened since Permian and Jurassic times! The scale of animal life has changed, less bone and muscle and more nerve and brains, less emphasis laid upon size and more upon wit. Only in the insect world are the dragons and monsters, and the carnival of blood and slaughter, repeated. In the shade of a summer tree, or in a clover-field, one may see minute creatures pursuing or devouring one another which, if enough times magnified, would rival any of the dragons of the prime.

XV. FAITH FOUNDED UPON A ROCK

I

PROBABLY that overwhelming calamity, the World War, set more good people adrift upon the sea of religious doubt and skepticism than all the accumulated evils of the past ten centuries. Men were everywhere outspoken in their want of faith in the Providence in which they had so long trusted. I heard of an English clergyman who declared that if the Germans won in the war he would never open his Bible again. Another English parson, with the thought of the war weighing upon him, published a volume of discourses which he called "The Justification of God." But judging from my own experiences with the book, the lay mind will find the grounds for justification as hard a riddle to read as the original one.

Only a faith founded upon the rock of natural law can weather such a storm as the world passed through in the Great War, but unfortunately such a faith is possible to comparatively few — the faith that the universe is radically good and beneficent, and that the evils of life grow upon the same tree with the good, and that the fruits called evil bear only a small proportion to those called good. Persons who do not read the book of nature as a whole, who do not try their faith by the records of the rocks and the everlasting stars, who are oblivious to the great law of evolution which has worked out the salvation of man and of all living things, through good and ill report, through delays and sufferings and agonies incalculable, but the issues of which have been unfailing, who do not see the natural universal order working in the fiery ordeal through which all nations during the historic period have passed, who have not learned that the calamities of men and of peoples are not the result of the wrath of some offended divinity, but the ups and downs in the long, hard road of human development, and that, in the nature of things, justice is meted out to all men — if not in a day, then in a year, or in a thousand years; if not to the individual, then to his family, or to his race — those who take no account of all these things soon lose their reckoning in times like ours.

Every good deed, every noble thought, counts in the counsels of the Eternal. Every bad deed, every ignoble thought, counts also. But the stream tends to purify itself; the world is thus made; evil is real, but short-lived; the remedial forces of life and nature burn it up or convert it into good. Our fertile landscapes are the result of the wear and tear of geologic ages; fire, flood, tornadoes, earthquakes, volcanoes, have all had a share in shaping them. Decay and death have fed the sources of life. Our own history as a people and the history of the European countries exhibit a like contrast and mingling of good and evil. We are too personal in our estimates, too limited in our perspectives; thoughts of our own comforts and private aims are too much with us. We must give Providence the advantage of a wiser perspective.

The thoughtful mind, capable of viewing these things on a bigger scale, does not need a world calamity to reveal the unsatisfactory character of the reigning gods. The daily course of events does that. Infantile paralysis, for example, with its long train of the crippled, unoffending children, or a man being slowly eaten up with cancer, or a mother losing her life in trying to save her child from flood and fire, and scores of other similar things, show what a thin veneer our theology puts upon ugly facts.

Our ecclesiastical faith must be housed in churches and kept warm by vestments. The moment we take it out into the open and expose it to unroofed and unwarmed universal nature, it is bound to suffer from the cosmic chill. For my part, I do not have to take my faith in out of the wet and the cold. It is an open-air faith, an all-the-year-round faith; neither killing frosts nor killing heats disturb it; not tornadoes nor earthquakes nor wars nor pestilence nor famine make me doubt for one moment that the universe is sound and good. The forces which brought us here and provided so lavishly for our sustenance and enjoyment; that gave us our bodies and our minds; that endowed us with such powers; that surrounded us with such beauty and sublimity; that brought us safely through the long and hazardous journey of evolution; that gave us the summer sun, the midnight skies, and the revolving seasons; that gave human love and fellowship and coöperation, childhood, motherhood, and fatherhood, and the sense of justice and mercy, are beneficent and permanent forces. They are directed to me personally because they are directed to all that live; they are the cause of the living, the

essence and the sum of all life of the globe. I do not
mind if you call them terrestrial forces; the terrestrial and the celestial are one. I do not mind if you
call them material forces; the material and the
spiritual are inseparable. I do not mind if you call
this view the infidelity (or atheism) of science;
science, too, is divine; all knowledge is knowledge of
God.

I have never taken shelter in any form of ec-
clesiasticism. I have never tried to clothe myself in
the delusive garments of a superstitious age. I have
never pinned my faith to a man-made God, however
venerable. I have inured my mind to the open air
of the universe, to things as they are, to the dealings
of a Power that exacts an eye for an eye and a
tooth for a tooth; a power that deals on the square.
Those apparent outlaws of the heavens, the comets,
do not disturb the naturist; sidereal space strewn
with dead worlds and burnt-out suns do not disturb him; the spectacle of the great planets rolling
through space void of life for untold millions of
years, does not disturb him; and if life should never
come to them, and should ultimately disappear from
the earth, he would not lose faith; he could behold
Europe drenched with the blood of a needless,
wicked war and not lose faith; he could see civilization retarded and the unjust cause triumph, and
still know that the Creative Energy has our good at
heart and always will have it.

II

THE demand of our day is for a scientific religion —
an attitude of mind toward creation begotten by
knowledge, in which fear, personal hopes, individual
good, and the so-called "other world," play little
part. Virtuous actions, upright conduct, heroic
character, the practice of the Golden Rule, are seen
to be their own reward, and the security of the
future is in well-doing and well-being in the present.
This is not religion in the old ecclesiastical sense,
but in the new scientific sense; a religion that moves
us to fight vice, crime, war, intemperance, for self-
preservation and in brotherly love, and not in obedience to theological dogma or the command of a God;
a religion that opens our eyes to the wonder and
beauty of the world, and that makes us at home in
this world. The old religion is a tree that has borne
its fruit. It is dying at the top; it is feeble at the
root. It no longer touches men's lives as of old. The
great things that are done to-day are not done in
the name of religion, but in the name of science, of
humanity, of civilization. The brotherhood that has
force and meaning is no longer a sectarian brotherhood; it is larger than all the churches combined.

The naturist must see all things in the light of his
experiences in this world. He experiences no miracles; he sees the cosmic energy as no respecter of persons; he sees the rains falling alike upon the just and

the unjust; he sees the vast, impartial, undiscriminating movements of Nature all about him; he learns that the land cannot sustain life without the fertilizing rains, yet he beholds the clouds pouring out their bounty into the sea just as freely as upon the land; he beholds the inorganic crushing the organic all about him, and yet he knows that the latter is nothing without the former.

If God and the universal cosmic forces are one, how surely is God on both sides in all struggles, all causes, all wars, righteous and unrighteous! We behold warring nations praying to the same God for victory; we see this same God now apparently favoring one side, now the other, and we are bewildered. Our theology takes us beyond soundings. But the naturist is not bewildered; he can read the riddle and reconcile the contradictions. Napoleon (if it was Napoleon) was right when he said that God was on the side of the heaviest artillery — the more power, the more God.

This may be a hard, chilling gospel; it is like going naked into the storm; but how can we deny it? Can we refuse to face it?

XV

THE POET OF THE COSMOS

THE world has had but one poet of the cosmos, and that was Whitman. His mind, his sympathies, sweep through a wider orbit than those of any other. I am bold enough to say frankly that I look upon him as the greatest personality — not the greatest intellect, but the most symbolical man, the greatest incarnation of mind, heart, and soul, fused and fired by the poetic spirit — that has appeared in the world during the Christian era.

In his lines called "Kosmos" he describes himself:

"Who includes diversity, and is Nature,
Who is the amplitude of the earth, and the coarseness and sexuality of the earth, and the great charity of the earth, and the equilibrium also,
Who has not look'd forth from the windows, the eyes, for nothing, or whose brain held audience with messengers for nothing,
Who contains believers and disbelievers, who is the most majestic lover,
Who holds duly his or her triune proportion of realism, spiritualism, and of the esthetic, or intellectual,
Who, having consider'd the body, finds all its organs and parts good,
Who, out of the theory of the earth, and of his or her body, understands by subtle analogies all other theories,
The theory of a city, a poem, and of the large politics of these States;

THE POET OF THE COSMOS

Who believes not only in our globe with its sun and moon, but in
       other globes with their suns and moons,
Who, constructing the house of himself or herself, not for a day
       but for all time, sees races, eras, dates, generations,
The past, the future, dwelling there, like space, inseparable to-
       gether."

Let me say at once that, whatever else "Leaves
of Grass" may be, it is not poetry as the world uses
that term. It is an inspired utterance, but it does
not fall under any of the usual classifications of
poetry. Lovers of Whitman no more go to him for
poetry than they go to the ocean for the pretty shells
and pebbles on the beach. They go to him for contact with his spirit; to be braced and refreshed by
his attitude toward life and the universe; for his
robust faith, his world-wide sympathies, for the
breadth of his outlook, and the wisdom of his utterances.

Whitman is first and last a seer and a philosopher,
but his philosophy is incarnated in a man; it is fluid
and alive; it breathes and talks, and loves and
breeds; it nurses the sick and wounded soldiers in
the hospitals; it makes him the friend and brother
of all types of humanity, of the outcast woman not
less than of the man or woman of perfect blood:

"Not till the sun excludes you do I exclude you,
Not till the waters refuse to glisten for you and the leaves to
       rustle for you, do my words refuse to glisten and rustle
       for you.

317

ACCEPTING THE UNIVERSE

"Whoever you are! you are he or she for whom the earth is solid
  and liquid,
You are he or she for whom the sun and moon hang in the sky,
For none more than you are the present and the past,
For none more than you is immortality."

My studies of nature and of the universe help me
to understand Whitman much more than does my
reading of literature itself.

Whitman is rapt and thrilled when he looks up
to the midnight sky. His very style is orbicular and
concentric. The scientific aspects of astronomy do
not engage him for a moment, any more than they
did the old Hebrew prophets; his science becomes
human emotion. He is the human soul matching
itself against the starry hosts, coping with them and
absorbing them:

"This day before dawn I ascended the hill and look'd at the
  crowded heaven,
And I said to my spirit, *When we become the enfolders of those orbs,
  and the pleasure and knowledge of everything in them, shall
  we be filled and satisfied then?*
And my spirit said, *No, we but level that lift to pass and continue
  beyond.*"

Is there not more than astronomy in these passages?

"I open my scuttle at night and see the far-sprinkled systems,
And all I can see multiplied as high as I can cypher edges but the
  rim of the farther system.

Wider and wider they spread, expanding, always expanding,
Outward and outward and forever outward.

My sun has his sun and round him obediently wheels,
He joins with his partners a group of superior circuit,
And greater sets follow, making specks of the greatest inside
them."

Again he says:

"It is no small matter, this round and delicious globe, moving so
exactly in its orbit for ever and ever, without one jolt, or
the untruth of a single second."

He is filled with "the great thoughts of space and
eternity," and common things assume new meanings in his eyes:

"I lie abstracted and hear the meanings of things and the reason
of things.
They are so beautiful I nudge myself to listen."

Who before Whitman ever drew his poetic, his
æsthetic, and ethical standards from the earth,
from the sexuality, from the impartiality of the
earth, or his laws for creations from the earth? Only
the wisest readers are prepared for their unliterary
flavor:

"I swear there can be no greatness or power that does not emulate those of the earth.
There can be no theory of any account unless it corroborates the
theory of the earth.
No politics, song, religion, behavior, or what not, is of account,
unless it compare with the amplitude of the earth,
Unless it face the exactness, vitality, impartiality, rectitude of
the earth."

We all see in Whitman, as we see in Nature, what
we bring the means of seeing. Readers of him are

likely to see their own limitations for the limitations of Whitman. It is as if we thought that the length of our sounding-line was the measure of the ocean's depth. It may be so, but it is not always so. A man of strict moral and ethical ideas, according to conventional standards, will find Whitman rank with original sin. Is not Nature rank with the same form of evil? Whitman did not shrink from natural tests. Naturalism was the essence of his religion.

" Nothing out of place is good, nothing in its place is bad."

But the good in Nature is vastly more than the evil, else you and I would not be here, and the good in Whitman is vastly more than the evil, or he would have been forgotten long ago.

Evil, as we use the term, attends all great things. Evil — some man's evil — comes out of the sunshine, the rains, the protecting snows. One of our poets objects to Whitman's saying that evil is just as perfect as good. Whitman does not say it is just as desirable, but just as perfect. Are not these things we call evil perfect — snakes, nettles, thorns, volcanoes, earthquakes? Is not a fungus as perfect as a rose? — a toad as perfect as a bird? Each obeys its own law. The germs of typhoid fever and of pneumonia are just as perfect as the germs that favor us. Whitman said:

"I permit to speak at every hazard Nature without check, with
original energy."

The hazards are great, but the stakes are great also. Readers who cannot stand an utterance of this sort should go to Pollock's "Course of Time," or Young's "Night Thoughts," or Dr. Holland's "Bitter Sweet."

Whitman bares his mind and soul to us as he bares his body. There are no masks or disguises. His inmost heart is as nude as his anatomy. Nothing is dressed up. No fashionable tailoring at all. There is nowhere the air of the studied, the elaborated. When other poets stand before the mirror, Whitman looks off at the landscape, or goes and bathes and admires himself. Or, to vary the image, when other poets distill perfumes, Whitman aims to give us the fresh breath of the unhoused air. In this respect he stands alone among modern English-speaking poets. He is the air of the hills and the shore, and not of a flower garden, or of a June meadow, or of parlors. That is what disappoints people. He aims at beauty no more than a wood or a river or a lake or a jungle does. His aim is to tally Nature.

It was my rare good fortune to know this quiet, sympathetic, tolerant man for more than thirty years, and to walk or saunter with him at all seasons and hours. Often at night he would stop and gaze long and silently at the stars, and then resume his walk. He was an easy-going, lethargic man — nothing strenuous about him, never in a hurry, never disturbed or excited, always in good humor, cleanly, clad in gray, with a fresh, florid complexion, large, broad, soft hands, blue-gray eyes, gray-haired and gray-bearded. He was fond of children and old people. What a contrast were his placid and easy-going ways to the astronomic sweep and power of his poems, his spirit darting its solar rays to the utmost bounds of the universe. When I was with him I did not feel his mighty intellect, I felt most his humanity, his primitive sympathy, the depth and intensity of his new democratic character, perhaps also that in him which led Thoreau to say that he suggested something a little more than human.

Whitman's attitude toward Nature stands out in contrast to that of all other poets, ancient or modern. It was not that of the poet who draws his themes from Nature, or makes much of the gentler and fairer forms of wood and field, spring and summer, shore and mountain, as has been so largely the custom of poets from Virgil down. Take all the Nature lyrics and idyls out of English and American poetry, and how have you impoverished it, how many names would suffer! Nor does Whitman's attitude in any degree conform to the worshipful attitude of Wordsworth and so many other poets since his time. He did not humanize Nature or read himself into it; he did not adorn it as a divinity; he did not see through it as through a veil to spiritual realities beyond, as Emerson so often does; he did not gather bouquets, nor distill the wild perfumes in his pages; he did not fill the lap of earth with treasures not her own — all functions of true poetry, we must admit, and associated with great names. Yet he made more of Nature than any other poet has done; he saw deeper meanings in her for purposes of both art and life; but it was Nature as a whole — not the parts, not the exceptional phases, but the total scheme and unfolding of things.

He sings more in terms of personality, of democracy, of nationalism, of sex, of immortality, of comradeship; more of the general, the continuous, the world-wide; more of wholes and less of parts, more of man and less of men. His religion takes no account of sects and creeds, but arises from the contemplation of the soul, of the Eternal, of the universe. We do not get the solace and the companionship with rural nature in Whitman that we get in the modern nature poets. With them we admire the "violet by a mossy stone," or the pretty shell on the seashore; with Whitman we saunter on the hills, or inhale the salt air of the seashore, or our minds open under the spread of the midnight skies — always the large, the elemental, the processional, the modern. The scholarly, the elaborated, the polished, the architectural, the Tennysonian perfume and technique, the Wordsworthian sweet rusticity and affiliation with fells and groves, the Emersonian mysticism and charm of the wild and the sequestered, were not for him or in him; nor the epic grandeur of

Milton, the dramatic power of Shakespeare, nor, usually, the lyric thrill of many of the minor poets. You embark on an endless quest with Whitman; not on a picnic, nor a "day off," but a day-by-day and a night-by-night journey through the universe:

"I tramp a perpetual journey,
My signs are a rain-proof coat, good shoes, and a staff cut from
    the woods.
No friend of mine takes his ease in my chair,
I have no chair, no church, no philosophy,
I lead no man to a dinner table, library, or exchange,
But each man and each woman of you I lead upon a knoll,
My left hand hooking you round the waist,
My right hand pointing to landscapes of continents and the
    public road,

Not I, not any one else can travel that road for you,
You must travel it for yourself."

He who can bring to Whitman's rugged and flowing lines anything like the sympathy and insight that beget them, will know what I mean. Our modern nature poets are holiday flower-gatherers beside this inspired astronomer, geologist, and biologist, all in one, sauntering the streets, loitering on the beach, roaming the mountains, or rapt and silent under the midnight skies. When, now, in my old age, I open his pages again and read the "Song of the Open Road," "Crossing Brooklyn Ferry," "The Song of the Broad-Axe," "This Compost," "Walt Whitman," "Great are the Myths," "Laws for Creation," and scores of others, I seem to be present at the creation of worlds. I am in touch with primal energies. I am borne along by a tide of life and power that has no parallel elsewhere in literature. It is not so much mind as it is personality, not so much art as it is Nature, not so much poetry as it is the earth, the sky. Oh, the large, free handling, the naked grandeur, the elemental sympathy, the forthrightness, and the power! Not beauty alone, but meanings, unities, profundities; not merely the bow in the clouds, but the clouds also, and the sky, and the orbs beyond the clouds. A personal, sympathetic, interpretive attitude toward the whole of Nature, claiming it all for body and mind, drawing out its spiritual and æsthetic values, forging his laws for creation from it, trying his own work by its standards, and seeking to emulate its sanity, its impartiality, and its charity.

Whitman wrote large the law of artistic productions which he sought to follow:

"All must have reference to the ensemble of the world, and the compact truth of the world;

There shall be no subject too pronounced — all works shall illustrate the divine law of indirections.

What do you suppose creation is?

What do you suppose will satisfy the Soul, except to walk free, and own no superior?

What do you suppose I would intimate to you in a hundred ways, but that man or woman is as good as God?

And that there is no God any more divine than Yourself?

And that that is what the oldest and newest myths finally mean?

And that you or any one must approach creations through such laws?"

ACCEPTING THE UNIVERSE

Whitman's standards are always those of Nature and of life. Emerson hung his verses in the wind — a good thing to get the chaff out of poetry or wheat. Whitman brings his, and all art, to the test of the natural, universal standards. He read his songs in the open air to bring them to the test of real things; he emulated the pride of the level he planted his house by. Always is his eye on the orbs, and on the earth as a whole:

> "I feel the globe itself swift swimming through space.
> I will confront the shows of day and night,
> I will see if I am to be less real than they are."

He would have his songs tally "earth's soil, trees, winds, waves."

"Can your performance face the open fields and the seaside?"

he demands of those who would create the art of America.

His poems abound in natural images and objects, but there is rarely a trace of the method and spirit of the so-called nature poets, some of whom bedeck Nature with jewelry and finery till we do not know her.

In one of his nature jottings, written in 1878 at his country retreat not far from Camden, New Jersey, he speaks thus of the emotional aspects and influences of Nature:

I too, like the rest, feel these modern tendencies (from all the prevailing intellections, literature, and poems) to turn everything to pathos, ennui, morbidity, dissatisfaction, death. Yet how clear it is to me that those are not the born results, influences of Nature at all, but of our own distorted, sick, or silly souls. Here amid this wide, free scene, how healthy, how joyous, how clean and vigorous and sweet!

I do not wonder that Whitman gave such a shock to the reading public sixty years ago. This return, in a sense, to aboriginal Nature, this sudden plunge into the great ocean of primal energies, this discarding of all ornamentation and studied external effects of polish and elaboration, gave the readers of poetry a chill from which they are not yet wholly recovered. The fireside, the library corner, the seat in the garden, the nook in the woods: each and all have their charm and their healing power, but do not look for them in Walt Whitman. Rather expect the mountain-tops, the surf-drenched beach, and the open prairies. A poet of the cosmos, fortified and emboldened by the tremendous discoveries and deductions of modern science, he takes the whole of Nature for his province and dominates it, is at home with it, affiliates with it through his towering personality and almost superhuman breadth of sympathy.

The egotism of Whitman was like the force of gravity, like the poise of the earth, the centrality of the orbs. Nothing could disturb it, no burden was too great for it to bear. He seemed always to have in mind the self-control and the *insouciance* of Nature.

He would fain try himself by the self-balanced orbs.
His imagination was fired by the undemonstrative
earth; he would be as regardless of observation as it
was. He was moved by the unsophisticated fresh-
ness of Nature. He saw that the elemental laws
never apologized; he would emulate the level he
planted his house by:

> "these shows of the day and night,
> I will know if I am to be less than they are."

He will not be outfaced by irrational things:

> "I will see if I have no meanings, while the houses and ships have
>   meanings,
> I will see if the fishes and birds are to be enough for themselves,
>   and I not to be enough for myself.
> I match my spirit against yours, you orbs, growths, mountains,
>   brutes,
> Copious as you are, I absorb you all in myself, and become the
>   master myself."

It is these cosmic and natural-universal standards
to which Whitman appeals, that mark him off from
all other poets or bards who have yet appeared, and
which, I hope, justify me in singling him out and
giving him a place in this volume.

THE END

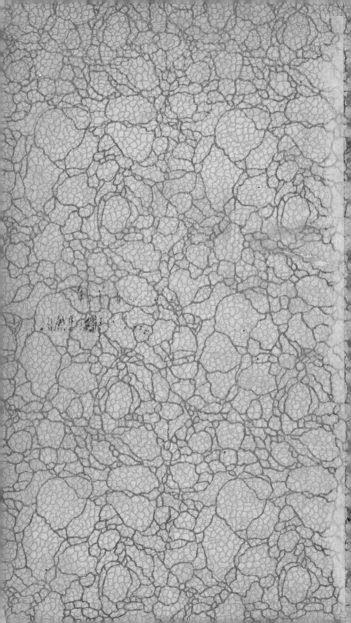